# A Walk-About in Australia

PHILIPPA BRIDGES

ETT IMPRINT

*Exile Bay*

This edition published by ETT IMPRINT, Exile Bay 2023

First published in 1925 by Hodder & Stoughton
This edition publishing Chapters 10 to 15 only of that edition

Copyright © ETT Imprint 2023

This book is copyright.

Apart from any fair dealing for the purposes of private study, research, criticism or review, as permitted under the Copyright Act, no part may be reproduced by any process without written permission. Inquiries should be addressed to the publishers.
ETT Imprint
PO Box R1906
Royal Exchange NSW 1225
Australia

ISBN 978-1-923024-32-8 (pbk)
ISBN 978-1-923024-33-5 (ebk)

Cover: Woman traveller in 1928

Design by Tom Thompson

# CONTENTS

1. Adelaide to Oodnadatta; Quorn, William Creek, Anna Creek, Oodnadatta, Macumba Station, meeting Topsy and the tracker Macumba Jack; Blood's Creek, Charlotte Waters, New Crown - - - - 7

2. Black Hill, Old Crown Point, Paddy's Plain, the Finke River, Horse Shoe Bend, Depot Sand-Hills, Alice Well, Wire Creek Soakage, Alice Spring - - - - 21

3. Simpson's Gap, Emily Gap, Alice Springs, Connor's Well, Ryan's Well, - - - - 34

4. Ti-tree Well, Central Mount Stuart, Hanson's Well, Stirling Station, Barrow Creek, Taylor's Well, Wycliffe Well, The Devil's Marbles, Tennant's Creek, - - - - 47

5. Tennant's Creek, Attack Creek, Banka Banka, Helen Springs, Powell's Creek, Newcastle Waters, Stuart's Plains, - - - - 58

6. MacGorey's Bore, Daly Waters, Number One Bore, Elsey Station, Maranboy, Rockhole, Five Mile Hole, Edith River, Pine Creek, to Darwin, - - - - 68

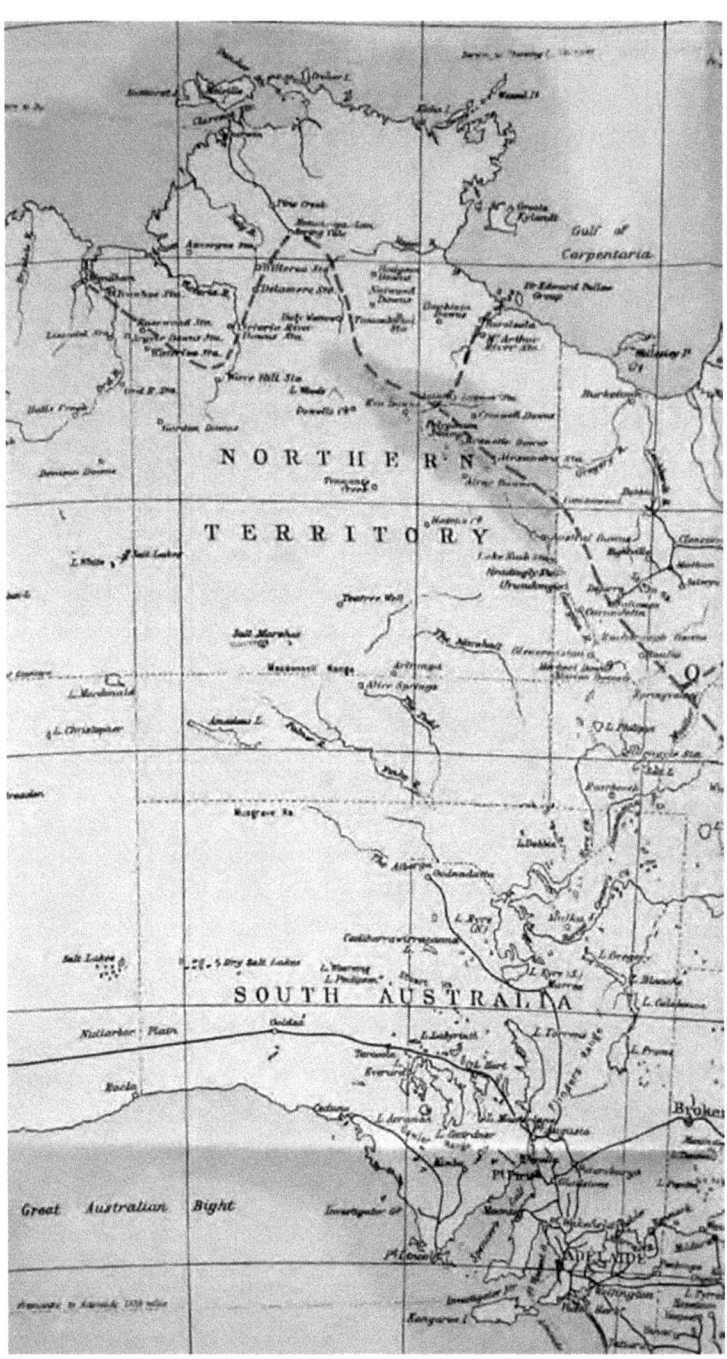

This map of the area Philippa Bridges travelled - north from Adelaide to Oodnatta, through to the Alice then on to Darwin; was published in 1925.

# 1

## TO CENTRAL AUSTRALIA

*The only distances in the world are those we carry within ourselves .-* PINERO.

A LONG enjoyable visit to my brother and sister-in-law at Adelaide was drawing to a close when the idea occurred to me of overlanding across the Continent and taking a homeward bound ship from Darwin. Central Australia has not so far attracted the woman traveller very much. The first lady to cross the Continent was Mrs. Dutton, who motored to Darwin from Adelaide with her husband a few years ago; and last year the Governor of Victoria and Lady Stradbroke followed the same route. I intended to travel unhurriedly in the same fashion as the dwellers themselves did. I had a great wish to see the Never-never, and possibly a flicker of the nomadic instinct may also have urged me, for I know that the thought of the long northward march, which extended practically from the great Australian Bight to the Arafura Sea, made a strong appeal. Before starting I talked with several people who had travelled in Central Australia, notably the Hon. Walter Duncan, who had recently returned from Darwin by motor, and Captain S. White, ornithologist and anthropologist, who has made several journeys into the heart of Australia, and whose wife has travelled farther by camel than any other white woman. It was from their conversation, coupled with my brother's account of his visit to the Northern Territory the year before, that I made my first mental picture of Central Australia.

Mr. Duncan's advice was given very humorously. "Remember on which side of the telegraph line you are, and if you meet with any real difficulty, make for it and damage it as much as you can! Then sit down under a telegraph pole and wait; somebody will be sure to come along."

I suggested that my rescuers might not be pleased to find the line broken, to which he answered, " It may be two or three days before they get to you, and by that time you won't be in a state to mind whether they are pleased or not!"

He told me how far I should have to travel with camels, where- the dreaded gastrolobium begins, at what stations I might expect to see a white woman, and other details.

One of Mrs. Dutton's many gifts is her " bushmanship," and she helped me in many ways, knowing exactly what I ought to take with me and what I could get on the way.

I left Adelaide on a cold spring day in August for Oodnadatta, by the fortnightly mail train, a thirty-six hours run of 686 miles. I found my fellow passengers congratulating themselves on having a through train, for until lately it was necessary to spend two nights on the way.

The Lower North is a renowned dairying district of which Quorn is the centre. The farms must be very large, for the homesteads are few, and upon all those undulating grassy slopes I did not see a cow.

Quorn Station was in darkness. We groped about after our baggage (for it is necessary to change carriages three times on the through train, partly on account of difference in gauge), one lantern among many, and partook of strong tea and meat pies, which seemed to be the only form of refreshment available. Presently a comfortable sleeping car was put on, in which one could have got a good night's rest had it not been for the incredible amount of bumping, which the other passengers accounted for by saying that cattle trucks had been coupled between the carriages, rendering the air-breaks useless.

An old lady of eighty-six, who had lived all her life in the Bush, and whom I was informed was a "pioneer," droving her own cattle, took the journey very easily. She sat bolt upright, eating meat pies with the best of us, remarking from time to time, " I likes travelling."

One of the men offered to bring us tea if we had anything to drink out of. I produced a miner's " quart pot" from my equipment.

"Can't beat the old quart pot," he said, and returned with a joram, remarking, " I am afraid it isn't very nice, for the water from the engine tastes so bad, but, anyhow, it's *wet*."

The dry salt country that bounds Lake Eyre is surely one of the thirstiest spots of the earth. There are glaring stretches of white pebbles encrusted with salt or soda, patches of yellow stone, patches of pink and lavender stone, but never a blade nor a shoot.

We may or may not have actually seen the lake that great brackish stretch of water that lies below the level of the sea and attracts, only to render useless, two good streams, the Cooper and the Diamantina. It seemed to lie quite near us to the east, which is its geographical position, but later it appeared to the north, and even north-west, and as mirage after mirage rose, playing a hundred tricks, we could not feel sure that we had seen the lake at all. All the delusions gradually resolved themselves into clumps of red-hot rock, that trailed slowly past the carriage window.

The train carried tanks of water to Oodnadatta and the railway cottages. There were several" bores" beside the line, simple-looking arrangements, by means of which a pipe, sunk to the level of the artesian basin (sometimes a depth of 2,000 feet), will send up a supply of water that appears to be unfailing. It may have a mineral or brackish taste, but it is always usable for stock, and able to support a little vegetation round the overflow. It is generally warm at the pipe, and sometimes almost boiling.

Water and occasionally cottages beside the line were the only interest. The rest of the landscape consisted of stones and stones and stones. They were mostly smooth pebbles, but here and there the sun would diamondize some little point which, if not a broken bottle, proved to be a wad of mica, which could be pulled into flakes with the fingers. Cornelians and garnets are found in certain districts.

At William Creek, still the same parched and shadeless country, the station master appeared with an invitation to dinner from his wife, and I spent a cool and pleasant hour with a gentle hostess, and discussed an excellent meal that made me forget the meat pies.

A deserted-looking spot called Anna Creek, about ten miles farther on, is the station for the Opal Fields, which lie about a hundred miles westward, where I am told there are plenty of opals, but trade is very slow because the stones are considered unlucky.

At Algebuckinna there was little water in the "river," and a dozen wild turkeys rose on one side of the line and a flock of sulphur-crested cockatoos on the other. Every traveller looks out for the Algy Bridge, because it is the longest in South Australia. Near here is a native burial ground, well known to doctors and anthropologists with predatory instincts.

Several fellow-passengers had introduced themselves, among them a retired sergeant of the fourth Dragoon Guards, who had made his home comfortably in Australia, and also a young police "trooper," who asked me to send a message to the Governor, who had helped him in his career, and he wished His Excellency to know how well he was getting on. He was now on his way from Port Augusta to Oodnadatta to bring back some "wild blacks," who had burgled a store somewhere out in the Never-never, the idea being that the man who was robbed was the first white man these natives had ever seen.

At night the air was cold and dry, with a tang which reminded one of Switzerland. I began to get an idea of the vastness of Australia as we journeyed along hour after hour, scarcely seeing a homestead, the sunset of dusky crimson, followed by. that pageant of orange, amber, amethyst, and jade that only a wide plain with a dry atmosphere can produce. Darkness came down like the shutting of a lid; there was a touch of frost in the air.

Somebody said that "George" would give us tea. George was the railway-gang cook at a halt. At "train-time" he was always ready with a plentiful supply of tea and pasties.

"You'll taste George's pasties," I was told, in a tone that made me think that a visit to Australia would not be complete without this experience. The train pulled up beside a low stone cottage, towards which there was a general exodus. I remained where I was, and presently a man came along with a simple invitation," He says, will you come?"

The courteous and hospitable cook and two or three of his friends were waiting at the door. They ushered me into the stone kitchen. A long table and forms were dimly lit by a swinging lamp that cast gleams and glooms on tired, good-humoured faces. The pasties and tea were really excellent. Then our host came rushing in to replenish the teapot, fell headlong over the end of a form, and beat a retreat. I hoped that he was not hurt, and his friends received this remark with something like indignation.

At the Macumba Station.

"A thing like that hurt *George*! George keeps himself in condition!"

Nevertheless, when we returned to the train George did not appear, and I am afraid that he had to nurse his bruises.

An hour later, in the pitch dark, we ran in Oodnanatta, and stopped at the platformless station, where the inhabitants were standing in a row two deep, awaiting the fortnightly excitement of the train.

I spent two or three days at Oodnadatta very pleasantly, thanks to the kindness and hospitality of Doctor and Mrs Shanahan. They have lived here for many years, and I found their conversation of unfailing interest.

There is no church at Oodnadatta or parson of any sort, but a Roman Catholic priest came by train for an annual three days' visit, and my hostess's drawing-room was turned into a chapel for Mass, confession, and a Christening.

Nominally the doctor's practice runs south, for it chiefly concerns the railway, but virtually it extends wherever a doctor is needed, and includes any sick person within reach, and several who might be considered out of reach. To the north there is no other medical man nearer than Darwin (about 1,300 miles).

Some years ago the telegraph brought news of a man hurrying doctorwards with lockjaw. He travelled by buggy with a herd of spare horses from a station 600 miles away, and was accompanied by two aborigines. His complaint made it impossible for him to eat, but his servants contrived in some fashion to make him swallow liquid food and orange juice. At night they camped and looked after him to the best of their ability, and in process of time - six weeks - they arrived at Oodnadatta. The Doctor, who had had news of him from the telegraph stations on the way, felt puzzled at the nature of the complaint, for he said that tetanus would have carried him off in about two days. He discovered that the jaws were locked owing to poison from a decayed tooth, and a cure was effected by chiselling away part of the bone. The patient made a good recovery, and then set off again with his natives on his 600-mile journey home.

This story of natives' devotion interested me very much, for I had been told that outside their tribal borders they are very unreliable, and I had been bade to consider the predicament I should be in if I woke up one morning in Central Australia and found that the natives had fled in the night, taking the camels and the water with them! People who understand their temperament say that a very small trifle may ruffle their feelings. A newcomer might not realize its importance, which they would be at a loss to explain, and they might think that the only way out of the difficulty was the shortest way home.

Oodnadatta holds a dance in the Memorial Hall on "train nights." On the wall hung the Roll of Honour. At the end of the room was a small stage with a drop scene painted by a local artist, with colours from his own Rock Pigment Works in the neighbourhood. Two buckets of clear, cold water stood on a table for the refreshment of the dancers.

Here linger dances that have been forgotten in English ballrooms: the polka, schottische, valita, and mazurka waltzes. The Master of Ceremonies stepped forward saying, " Gents, select your partners for the Alberts," and I watched a quadrille-like measure that I suppose Queen Victoria must have trod with the Prince Consort.

A day or two later I went on to the Macumba, one of the cattle stations of Sir Sidney Kidman, who had very kindly offered to help me on my journey.

My first experience of station life was at the Macumba, and it proved a very pleasant one. The comfortable homestead consisted of two small houses linked together by a covered passage. A lawn of buffalo grass and a few green trees made a point where the eye could rest. The surrounding country was of a cornelian variety of rock called" gibbah," generally small pebbles of a brilliant crimson, massed together as tightly as if they had been rolled. A clear sunset in the dry season with a rosy afterglow defies description. The road from Oodnadatta, by way of Trooper's Hole and Tar Creek, had been made with an implement like a snow plough that cleared away the loose stones.

I began to realize the spaciousness of Australia when Mr. Kempe, the manager, told me that he managed 12,000 miles of cattle stations. In reply to my question, " How many beasts to the acre?" he said, " Acre? None to the acre; about one and a half to the square mile."

He made the preparations for the first part of my journey, with the result that I had a very compact little "plant," efficient and easy to handle. The four camels were in charge of a native boy called Macumba Jack, whose lubra (wife), y-clept Topsy, came as my maid. There were the necessary saddles, harness, camel boxes, and other gear. Mrs. Kempe packed a capacious and well-filled tucker-box, and Mr. Kempe saw to it that I had a new, strong, and comfortable saddle.

Having said good-bye to the Macumba party, and thanked my host and hostess most heartily for their hospitality and kindness in making such careful arrangements, I mounted my camel, was heaved aloft, and set off, Mrs. Kempe's parting advice being, "Whish down well before sunset, and get a comfortable camp before dark."

Mrs Dutton with her Dodge Brothers car on her 1921 trip.

Rain had been threatening all day, and postponed my departure until after dinner, so the first stage was a short one of about twelve miles. We camped at Ross's Hole, and though I got in before nightfall, nothing could have made it a comfortable camp, for the wind rose, bringing the dust, which smothered everything, and nearly scattered the fire. Most of the creeks and holes had dried up, for this season bade fair to be the worst for forty years, which in this country means within the memory of man. I settled down under the lee of my tent, opened the excellent tucker-box, and ate my evening meal. Macumba Jack and Topsy, their work in camp finished, had settled down under a break-wind of branches, and were cheerfully making the best of things. On the other side of the muddy water hole the camels were vigorously breaking off branches of the gum-trees and eating the leaves.

By morning the whole camp seemed to be buried in dust. It came almost like rain, and as fast as it was shaken or brushed off, it collected again. The blacks felt the cold bitterly, and rode along with their blankets over their heads. At the Ten Mile I dismounted to look at the Bore, and found scalding hot water tumbling out of a pipe, making a small lake with its outrush, the cooler end of which harboured a splendid flock of waterfowl. An iron hut, the only building for many miles, appeared to be a store, for it was full of tinned oysters; and a white man whom Macumba Jack called Ole Ike Hervey shook my dusty hand in his dusty hand, and wished me the best of luck. The only other living thing that I saw that day was an emu, which would not wait to be photographed, but raced away with enormous strides faster than a horse can gallop. We camped about sunset at Aldnagowra, and during the night the wind abated.

In the morning we met the camel mail that plies between Oodnadatta and Horse Shoe Bend on its return journey. The mailman, Mr. Bromley, whished down his camel, and the string came to a standstill.

He told me that there was no feed within six miles of Hamilton Bore, for it had all been eaten out by cattle. The camel mail struck me as being a strange and picturesque survival. Probably its days are numbered, for as soon as the heavy sandy creek called the Alberga is bridged for motors, a car will be able to run all the way to Alice Springs, with little fear of getting" bogged" in the sand. At present the mail service of Central Australia is not very adequate. Alice Springs gets a fortnightly camel mail from Oodnadatta, the "rail head," but the stations beyond are served once in six weeks, which, of course, means that they only have regular communication with the outer world eight times in the year.

A few hours later, when the lubra and I were riding along, the boy making a circuit through the woods in search of game, we came upon a lost bull camel, and Topsy cried, "I frightened he go for us." So we took the string into the Bush, whished down and dismounted, and when he came towards us I flapped a big cloak at him, and Topsy waved a long pole, and though he returned again and again, our united wavings and flappings persuaded him at last to depart. He had a broken hobble on his leg, and looked a very derelict ship of the desert; but he was dangerous as well as pathetic, and answered to Kipling's description, "A devil and an ostrich and an orphan child in one." We had dinner in a little dry creek near the road, and a black boy on a trotting camel swung into view, looking for the bull, which he said had got away from the mail two days ago. He had dinner with my blacks, and then, though they told him that the camel was not far off, he departed the way he had come, saying he would "send nother black fellah."

At Hamilton Bore, which we reached about 4 o'clock, there was a large Afghan encampment with about a hundred camels, and the land was as bare of grass as if it had been ploughed and harrowed. There was a dead cow in the water, but nobody seemed to mind, and as Macumba Jack did not see his way to pulling it out, we left it there.

Our four camels were all strong animals individually, but they did not make a good string, camels being more difficult to match than pearls, for the excellence of the string lies not in the equal or graduated size of the units, but in their ability to walk at a regulation pace. Barley and Snowy, the lead and baggage camels, could do a steady three miles an hour all day long, and my riding camel and the Oont were both good trotters, though slow walkers. Barley had suffered rough handling at some time in her life, for part of her nostril had been torn away, and a new place pierced for the stud. On the afternoon march she carried the baggage, and Snowy, released from the load and made leader, began to walk too quickly, with the result that I noticed Barley's nose was bleeding, and called a halt.

"Camels always like that," said Macumba Jack. "Got maggots in their nose. I could have shown you this morning."

I was not in the mood for investigations of this description, however. I had been in the saddle for many hours, and had got to the pitch when one wonders which part of the camel's stride is the most trying, the jerk or the sway. During the sway one thinks that it is the sway, but when the jerk comes one is convinced that it is the jerk. The discovery about Barley's nose and the repulsive conversation concerning the maggots warned me that it was time the day's march came to an end. I whished down, dismounted, and said I would lead Barley for a mile or two, and set off towing her along as gently as I could.

The sun had gone, and the crimson sky was reflected upon the" gibbah," so that the whole world was the tint of a ruby. A sharpness came into the air, and darkness descended rapidly. I would have camped an hour ago but that the" gibbah " offered us no feed, and even two or three miles farther on, when some rough scrubby stuff appeared that the boy said was good camel tucker, we still had to continue the march in search of wood.

But let those who set out upon a long camel journey take heed when Nature gives the word to halt. About seven o'clock two or three dead trees stretched out black arms against the purple gloom, and hailing them only as firewood, regardless of their picturesque effect, we whished down, and set to work to pitch camp. And I went to my tent, feeling very sick on this, my third day aboard the ship of the desert.

We had had a twenty-seven mile march, and I shall remember Jacuna as a Dantesque, end-of-the-earth-looking spot, which the black gable of my tent and a few red embers seemed to strive almost in vain to bring it within the inhabited portion of the globe.

The next day we did only a short stage, and I chose to walk. The camels had all recovered, and were in good form, though the stony country had only yielded a feed of dry stalks.

In the afternoon we came to a little dry creek, and I was suddenly aware of a great longing for the shade, so I called to Topsy, who was leading, "I tired. Stop here; lie down; sleep one hour," and I pulled a thick coat off the load, rolled up in it, and promptly suited the action to the word. An hour later the boy shuffling his feet among some dry sticks to wake me, remarked, "Suppose you like stop, make good camp, done two days' hard travelling!" So we encamped for the night, and just before sunset some little red-breasted swifts appeared, apparently catching flies in the air under a gum-tree. As soon as the sun set it became very cold, and I was glad to have a good fire, but the air was very exhilarating. This wonderful dry air should cure all the chest complaints in the world, but I only saw one person taking advantage of it, an ex-soldier who lived in a tent at Oodnadatta on the Crown land, which is free to all.

At these dry camps between waters it is a little difficult to find out the name of the locality. The boy called this the Half Caste's Grave, because, he said, there was a half-caste woman buried under stones near the road.

Blood's Creek, called after a Doctor Blood who once travelled this way, proved a hospitable spot in spite of its arid surrounding and uneuphonious name. Mr. and Mrs. Roper, who have a hotel and store here, came out to meet me with a hearty reception.

"Just where you are standing now," Mr. Roper said, "His Excellency the Governor stood, and talked to us all as if we had been his equals." (This was on the Governor's journey to Central Mount Stuart in connection with the proposed railway.) I was invited to stay the night, but felt it was 'too early in the journey to tarry. There was a large party at dinner, nine in all, from various remote places. I had a comfortable rest and a pleasant chat with Mrs. Roper, who gave me several hints on Bush travel, and also remarked, "I think you will feel you have had enough of it by the time you get to Alice Springs."

We watered the camels, filled up the canteens, and started off

Macumba Jack in Afghan town, Oodnadatta.

The Camel Mail.

again in the burning heat, across the sand and the gibbah.

During the afternoon I came upon the boy dismounted, hat in hand, looking down at a little heap of stones.

"He bin perish," he said. "Some man bin perish. Dunno who. Dunno when, but he planted there."

I would not have known that the place was a grave, and asked if there was a white man buried there, and the boy said yes, he knew by the stones. To "perish," in these parts, means to die of thirst. The boy mounted again with a sigh, as if of regret that anyone should perish in a place where life is as scarce as it is here.

Next day we crossed the undefined border of the Northern Territory, and arrived at Charlotte Waters, another arid spot reached after a long pilgrimage across the gibbah.

The telegraph station is built of solid blocks of stone, with a walled courtyard, designed for defence; relic of the old troublous days when the natives still hoped to exterminate the white men. Indeed, it was not until some of the aborigines had paid visits to the cities of the south that they gave up the hope of doing so, the population of the cities convincing them that the white man had come to stay.

Mr. Hocking, the station master, said that he had expected me to dinner. "I had a hot roast waiting for you until two," he said. I asked him how he knew that I was coming, and he said that Mrs. Roper had told him on the telephone that at the pace I was travelling I should be at Charlotte Waters in time for dinner.

It was refreshing to sit in a cool room and drink tea, for there was not a particle of shade on the road.

Then I crossed the hot dry creek that I suppose in the wet season is Charlotte Waters, to see Mrs. Johnson, whose husband was just completing the new well. They were living in a tent, and Mrs. Johnson told me that tent-life was quite comfortable until the wind began to blow, when the dust distracted her. In that little canvas home she seemed to have everything necessary to civilized life.

She asked me if I was not lonely travelling with only black servants, and seemed surprised when I told her that I had not felt at all lonely so far, but might have been so if I had not had a good lubra with me. She asked me to camp beside her, but this I was not able to do, for there was no feed for several miles round the well, and I thought it wiser to stay with the camels. There were several people working here, and the big iron tank and engine and rigging gave an air of progress that I had not seen before on the journey.

It was now dark, and we had four miles on heavy sand before we could find anything that the camels could eat. Then it was gidgea, a tough, drought-resisting, woody bush with pointed leaves and a profusion of yellow flowers. Dead bullocks, a frequent roadside feature, had begun to appear again, and I dreaded that in the dark we should camp upon their bones. The boy and lubra, though anxious to get to their supper and rest, were very patient. They lit the lantern and searched over the ground, reporting, "No bones here, Aracucha. No dead bullock. Good clean camp."

My efforts at bird study were rather disappointing at first. As it was springtime I had expected to find birds pairing and nesting, but this was not the case. It seems that they build their nests after rain, whatever time of year it falls, for it is only then that they can get food for their young.

There were many nests by the way, about as big as that of our thrush, built of twigs, thickly plastered with mud. Topsy said they were the nests of a tiny finch-like bird akin to the diamond sparrow. They looked very durable, and were evidently intended either to resist much rain, or else to solve the housing problem for more than one season.

I saw several kinds of hawks, which are beautiful, graceful birds in spite of their bad reputation, large flocks of galah parrots and sulphur-crested cockatoos, and occasionally a pair of Major Mitchells. Live rabbits were scarce, but we frequently came upon dead ones, stuck in the lower branches of trees, whither they must have climbed in search of food only to get entangled and perish.

We reached New Crown, one of Sir Sidney Kidman's stations, during the afternoon. There was much here that was interesting. Some camels were being broken in to "buggy work," and a team of six was tear-

tearing round the station with a heavy waggon in tow, accompanied by a little crowd of natives. Mr. King, the manager, showed me the garden and well, and some horses that he was feeding by hand, in order to have something that would carry him. The stockyard contained a useful contrivance called a "crush-gate," by means of which one horse can be separated from a mob and shut up in a tiny "box" made of rails. He also showed me some fascinating little dingo pups, the first I had ever seen, and gave me good counsel regarding my journey, advising me, since I was "travelling happily" with my present plant, not to change it at Alice Springs, but to take it on as far as possible. He also remarked that there was no such thing as accuracy in the Bush. "If you ask ten Bushmen the same question, you will get ten different answers."

The moment the sun set a cold wind arose, as keen as if it blew across some snow-capped sierra. Every now and then there was a rush of galloping hoofs as a mob of Bush horses went by to the well to drink. I had not stayed near a well before, and these rushes gave a very individual touch to the evening. It was too dark to see them, but I had the impression that horses came by the hundred. The manager kindly offered to lend me a "fed" horse, but there would have been difficulties about food and water, so it was better to stick to the camels. The season was so terribly dry that the ship of the desert was far the best means of transport.

# 2

*O man, hold thee on in courage of soul*
*Through the stormy shades of thy worldly way,*
*And the billows of cloud that around thee roll*
*Shall sleep in the light of a wondrous day.*
  - SHELLEY

AFTER leaving New Crown I camped about four miles south of Black Hill. During the night a penetrating wind again arose, and I awoke to find my tent blowing about in the most uncomfortable way. I called up Topsy to bring something heavy to keep the edges down, and my two retainers instantly came running with the two water canteens, which seemed to answer the purpose. I tried to sleep and to ignore the noise of the wind, but presently I heard a "gurgle-gurgle," and was disgusted and even alarmed to find that the wind had capsized one of the canteens, which had been left uncorked, and the water was pouring away merrily. I managed to prop it up, but a moment later a lull in the wind brought another "gurgle-gurgle" from the other canteen, which was pouring out its contents in the same fashion. While I was trying to cope with the situation, my tent blowing about my head none too gently the while, I remembered Mrs. Roper's words, "I think you will have had enough of camping out by the time you get to Alice Springs."

Happily there was enough water left for breakfast, and we were only half a day's march from Old Crown Well. Otherwise it might have been a serious matter, and any trouble would have been entirely my own fault, for I had repeatedly been warned that natives are "forgetful children," and I had neglected to see that they had corked up the canteens after the quart pots had been filled for supper.

These canteens hold four gallons each. They are carried on the front of the camel saddle, slung on with hobbles. My small valise on top of them, and a rider, made just a light load for a riding camel. They are made of galvanized iron, strongly strapped with the same metal, and slightly curved to fit against the animal's sides. The pattern is as old as the hills the ancient Egyptians having proved its practical value. The hobble straps are made of green hide (untanned bullock hide), buttoned with a big Turk's head knot. They are extremely strong, but this untreated leather becomes very hard, and is apt to rub the animal's feet.

Most of the wells in the Dead Heart are leased to settlers who undertake to keep them in repair and charge stockmen a small sum per head for mobs of cattle and horses watering there.

All the country round the Old Crown Station was terribly parched. The horses were too weak to work, and only camels and donkeys were now being used. Mr. Summerfield at the Old Crown Well is said to have the best camels in Australia. They certainly looked in excellent condition, and reflected great credit upon their owner. The difficulties of life in these parts can be a little imagined when one hears of donkey teams being sent several miles for firewood, and one knows that every sort of foodstuff, save meat alone, must be brought by pack animal from Oodnadatta. Mr. and Mrs. Summerfield kindly invited me to dinner, talked about the problems of life in the country, and showed me strange pebbles and "rubies" found on the hill-sides near by.

The vegetation was withered, the grass burnt up.

All plants and trees were of the passive resister sort that clings desperately to life, sets its teeth to endure privation, and becomes gnarled and woody, or else prickly and wiry, in the attempt. Some of the settlers are wont to speak of themselves as battlers, but it seemed to me that the herbage had also to develop fighting instincts in order to live.

Old Crown Point is a steep round hill, whose shape must have suggested its name: It lies about three miles beyond the Summerfield homestead. The rock is of all colours of the rainbow. It is locally called "paint-stone," and probably ochres could be got from it. In one place a landslide had left a great patch of lavender-coloured shale, and there were many curious effects.

I had hoped to get both a breeze and a view from the top of the hill, but it was a difficult climb, for the overhanging" crown" is about twenty feet high, and even the ascent to it was not easy, the rocks being so loose that they came away almost at a touch. So I gave it up, and after

Aboriginal camel handlers, Oodnadatta (top);
Mr & Mrs Summerfield, of the Old Crown Well (left);
Crossing the Finke River, about 1922 (below).

a couple of hours' wandering, having gathered some bits of wolfram and stones that I hoped were garnets, I struck out towards the road. The camels were nowhere in sight, but it was a still day, and a few shouts brought an answer, and they presently came into view, dawdling along leisurely under the gum-trees.

I was never afraid of losing myself on my little excursions, for the Australian aboriginal is a tracker above all else - I believe he can see a footprint on a bare rock - and I felt sure that Jack and Topsy would always have found me. Tracking is part of an infant's early education. As soon as a child can crawl its mother takes a paw of wallaby or 'possum, and gives him lessons in reading footprints in the dry sand. Topsy sometimes amazed me by looking down from the height of the camel-saddle and remarking, "Dingo, three days old;" "Kangaroo, last night;" "Snake, this morning." I once hoped to floor her by asking which way did the snake go, but she answered promptly, "That way." I learnt to know the track of a snake, but never got to the pitch of being able to tell in which direction it was travelling. I had become so used to flat scenery that Old Crown Point was quite notable, and it stood out well in the landscape for many a mile after we had said good-bye to it.

The look of the country changed again. Coloured stones became things of the past, and on all sides appeared queer crinkled black rocks, and sometimes rounded slabs of stone like huge broken bits of pottery.

I camped on Paddy's Plain after darkness had fallen.

Topsy had to make damper and flap-jack, which she did very neatly. Her pasty board was a sack sprinkled with flour, on which she kneaded the dough made of flour, baking-powder and water. Meanwhile, the boy had got a good hot wood fire, and Topsy beat the charcoal into tiny pieces, and mixed it with earth to lessen the heat, then she threw on the damper, and covered it carefully with a mixture of charcoal and earth, putting embers on the top. She baked the flap-jacks on the embers without covering them. They were done in a few minutes, but the damper took two hours to bake.

In the morning we saw Old Crown Point again for many miles. It looked quite imposing, its queer shape easily recognized. All the little hills and headlands have flat tops, as if Nature endeavoured to bring everything down to the same level. There are "ranges," or rather tongues, of land stretching at intervals for about thirty miles south-west at Crown Point.

When the hill had gradually faded from view, there was nothing to look at except the usual flatness, the stunted gums, mulga, and sometimes gidgea, pinbush and bogobine grass.

The crossing of the Finke, which we traversed twenty-five times in all, made a pleasant diversion. Of course, there was no water, just hot, coarse, dry sand, but the beautiful gum-trees with white trunks and young green leaves harboured many birds, and the foliage was not dusty like that of the trees on the plains. The eucalypts have a fascination of their own. They also are battlers, and as it is very necessary for them to conserve moisture, Nature has taught them to hang their leaves downwards.

Unfortunately for the traveller, this vertical foliage gives the minimum of shade.

Shortly after midday I reached Horse Shoe Bend, descending a steep, chalky track among curious heaps of rock and rubble, which looks like the refuse of mines, though the boy told me they are really the work of Nature ("No man done it"). The Finke River has christened the place by making a curve round it in the shape of a horseshoe. Mr. and Mrs. Elliot, who have their home and a hotel here, kindly invited me to stay, but as there is never any feed for animals near a well, a great deal of time has to be spent in leading them out to graze and fetching them back again, so I felt obliged to continue the journey in the afternoon, though I regretted not being able to accept Mrs. Elliot's very cordial invitation.

The Finke Creek was scorchingly hot when we watered the camels, and I was glad to leave the glare of the white sand and get on to the Hugh River, where there are lovely gum-trees, and as the afternoon waned, we reached the Depot Sand-Hills, camping about four miles south of Rocky Hill. The sand was as red as brick dust, and the camels floundered about in it. We went up and down some steep rises.

Topsy alighted and caught a sand-devil, a little animal that looked like a large toad, but walked like a lizard, and was clothed in a patchwork of small squares, each with a soft but prickly spine. It carried its little" swag" on its bag, and thrust out its head from a sockety neck like that of a tortoise. It seemed to have no weapon of defence but to make faces. After I had had a good look at it, Topsy put it down again, and it walked into hiding between two inadequate stalks. Later we saw others sitting at the mouths of their tunnels, waiting for us to go by. They all seemed ridiculously tame.

The gum-tree likes a hard bed for its roots, so none grow in the sandhills. The beautiful casuarina, locally called the "oak," holds sway. It is at its best in "soft" country, and I suppose from its long, depending needles with many joints, that it is a beautiful amplification of the ugly little weed called marestail. There are, I believe, twenty varieties of casuarina, including the she-oak, bull-oak, and beefwood.

Throughout my whole trip I had no more lovely camp than that in the Depot Sandhills. The wind was cold enough to make me glad of a tent, and the natives built a big fire.

It was a clear night, with many stars; the Southern Cross tilted over sideways, and Orion looked very remote. A light wind moved among the casuarinas, and when it stopped the needles continued to sway with the sound of waves upon the beach. Wind among gum-trees is seldom restful, for it generally brings a dust-devil, or "whirlie," which makes a disturbing roar like a train in a tunnel, but a capful of breeze among the casuarinas turns the whole of the Depot Sandhills into a melody.

At Alice Well Constable Mackay at the police station gave me dinner, talked about the country and native life, and cleverly mended the camera, which had been jolted out of action. He showed me a tree in the Creek marked "D. I. G.," with an arrow, to show the direction the water lay, the work of a telegraphist as long ago as 1872. The Overland Telegraph from Darwin to Adelaide is about fifty years old, and the laying of it across the Continent must have been a wonderful feat. The

A donkey team in the far north of South Australia.

A donkey team in the Territory moving an immense hay bale.

us a short cut through the Bush, saving twenty-two miles, or about a day's travelling, and this I decided to do, partly because time was a consideration, but also out of curiosity to know what a "black-fellah road" was like. As a matter of fact, there was no road at all, we just struggled along through the Bush for eight hours, and I am sure that both camels and riders found it much more tiring than the proper road would have been. Camels like a pad along which they can follow each other dreamily, and the Bush seemed to make them all nervous; the rider had to be on the alert the whole time. I rode the Oont, which was quite a good little camel and a fine trotter, but when it came to getting through a thicket, instead of letting me choose the place, he would rush at it, put his head down, and scrape through somehow. Of course, I got scratched and torn. Upon the road the Oont would never have dreamt of jumping a gutter across the pad, but out in the Bush he leapt these gutters in an amazing fashion, and he would rush at a wash-away, and scramble through it in a manner quite different from his usual cautious behaviour. Then he would tear on until we came to another obstacle, which he would negotiate with a rush or a scramble or a leap. It was late in the afternoon when we emerged from the thickets on to the proper track.

I camped early, feeling that I had had enough exercise. Topsy, who was a most industrious lubra, made the damper, and then cut out and began stitching a new dress that she intended to make.

By taking the "black-fellah road" we had unfortunately missed Maryvale Station, the home of Mr. and Mrs. Hayes, upon whom I should like to have called. Though I seldom felt lonely, either during the day's march or the solitary evenings in camp, it was, of course, always a pleasure and an event to arrive at a homestead.

After the day's skirmishing about the camels were quite ready for a good drink of water at Deep Well the next morning, and here I found news from Adelaide, to which I was able to reply, Deep Well being in telephone communication with the telegraph station.

Topsy was a picture of industry, perched upon her camel, stitching away at her new dress to be "flash" to enter Alice Springs.

I had run out of meat, and told the boy to try to shoot a bird. But we saw nothing edible. After a sudden halt, however, and a race round a bush with a stick, he came running with a lizard that he had caught. He carried it along in a kerosene tin, and cooked it in the ashes of the fire for dinner. It was very tender, and tasted like chicken. I think it was the species they call iguana. The native name is *drazda*.

I was surprised at the way meat kept fresh in this burning weather. It was unpacked every night, and laid on a branch to cool, but all through the day it travelled along wrapt up in cloths in the tucker-box, with the sun pouring down upon the lid. One of my kind wayside friends, however, told the boy to gather gum leaves and lay them on the top of the box with a thick sack over them, and this must have helped to keep the larder cool.

The blacks eat a great deal of meat. For their morning lunch they would share a lump of beef about as big as a football, despatching it without any bread. Their dinner was always a serious matter, and I never knew that human beings could eat so much, for when they had finished a large ration of beef, they would turn their attention to three or four rabbits and half a dozen galahs that they had killed on the morning's march. We frequently killed snakes, but all of one variety-the alinga. If there was a chance of cooking a snake immediately, the natives would always enjoy eating it, but they would never eat one that had been killed for more than about an hour.

I got the idea that we were losing time, and decided upon a night march, so we camped from 5.30 to 7.30, and I had a supper of parrots. Though not a good shot, the boy was an excellent hunter. I used to watch him stalking game. He got quite close to it before risking a shot from his short-barrelled gun. If he got three parrots for the expending of one cartridge it was all the better, though I always felt a little compunction at killing these beautiful little birds for food, especially as they did not make a very satisfactory meal.

It was beautiful riding along under the stars. The camels watched the road intently, every hair on the alert, and picked their way with care over the shadows even of twigs. Macumba Jack preferred to walk, so he tied his camel to the tail of Snowy, and set off into the Bush. I think he had an idea of hunting, but about an hour later he returned to the string, and said he would lead. Both he and Topsy slept while they were riding, and I felt so drowsy that I kept" dropping off" also, but waking with a sudden start as Ladybone skipped over a dark shadow I suddenly realized that I might be in danger of dropping off in another fashion, and after that I kept watch. The Bush was such a place of beauty and interest under the faint light of the stars that I was loth to call a halt at all, but about midnight fatigue compelled me to do so, and we whished down, unloaded, hobbled the camels with all swiftness, and sent them off to graze, I helping with the work. The boy searched the ground with tufts of lighted grass, reporting, " No snake - all clean." Topsy threw my sleeping-bag on to the ground, and the next instant I was asleep. I do not think, however, that we saved much time by the night march, for my retainers were very dull and slow in the morning.

Wire Creek Soakage, to which Macumba Jack had often alluded, proved to be an unimpressive hole in a mud bank. Nevertheless, if we had been short of water, it would have been of the utmost importance, for we could have procured it here by digging. The boy shot rabbits, parrots, and a bird that I identified as the Papuan frogmouth. I asked, " What does he say?" and the blacks both answered "Ooom, ooom," which tallies with the description in Leach's " Bird Book."

The day grew hotter and hotter; there was no shade whatever, only hot brown earth and a few brown rusty trees. The distant rim of hills towards which we were travelling lost their morning blueness and became barren and arid. They were the Macdonnell Ranges, and presently the boy pointed out Emily Gap to the east, and the conical hill that appears to block the passage through the Ranges to Alice Springs.

I seldom met a soul; there were not many passers-by in the Dead Heart. The Myalls or "Bush blacks" have retreated farther and farther into the Bush in search of water and game as one after another the creeks, claypans, and waterholes dry up. Natives who are in touch with whites had come into the stations where they received Government rations (a little flour, tea, and possibly sugar), and the bones of beasts killed for food were also given to them.

These blacks were not prepossessing to look at ; either they wear far too many clothes, or else none at all. They sleep behind a breakwind called a whirlie, or sometimes in a humpy made of branches, old sacks, or something equally unromantic. The boy's efforts to find a shady place for the dinner

Picnic at Simpson's Gap, with Topsy and Jack.

Meeting the mailman by Herbert Basedow, 1923.

camp were in vain, so he chopped down two or three small trees as an impromptu shelter.

During the afternoon a Myall suddenly stepped out of the Bush in front of us, and it was so long since the Oont had seen a passer-by that he went off at full gallop. He raced along for about half a mile, and as it would have been very difficult to pull him up without pulling out the nose stud, by which means alone the Australian camel is controlled, I let him go, and made the discovery that a camel's fast gallop is a far easier pace than his walk. Animals that are used to travelling through the Bush get very shy, and will look with deep suspicion upon anyone else who has the assurance to use His Majesty's highway!

The sun was at its very hottest that afternoon after the episode was over. As I was riding at the tail of the procession I saw Topsy's camel sway across the road followed by Barley, and then Ladybone, carrying Jack, began to walk solemnly round a bush. "Don't come very near, please - snake here," said Jack, as I rode up. I said that I would like to see it, and was told that it had gone into a "mice's hole."

We whished down and began digging with sticks round the roots of the bush, but found nothing. I said it must have got away, but the blacks, whose eyes are as keen as the eyes of the wild things, said that it was still there, so I told them to get it, and retired to a small patch of shade under a tree. The heat was enough to cook one. Presently they called out that they had found it.

"Please stand alonga Topsy. I chuck him," and the boy dug the snake out with a stick and" chucked" it into the air. Topsy squealed, "I frightened," which was her way when there were snakes about, but she helped to get some bits of wood, nevertheless, which we threw at him to engross his attention while the boy got a strong stick, the snake dabbing hither and thither meanwhile. The method of killing the snake is to give one good blow on the head, and then to pat its back all the way down to the tip of its tail and up again. After this the boy took it by the tail and swung it round in the air many times, finally banging it so hard upon the ground that the head flew off.

I examined the head. The boy seemed to understand a good deal about it, and showed me the "poisoned teeth" and the way that they come forward when the jaws are opened, and the hollow tubular tongue. They carried the alinga along with them, and I believe subsequently ate it.

As the sun grew low we wended our way across a very parched bit of country. Apparently we were nearing Alice Springs. The boy kept pointing with his hand and saying, "Close up - close up," but there was no sign of a habitation. The Macdonnell Ranges were not so imposing as they had been a few hours ago. They seemed only to add to the barrenness of the landscape. Presently a white man came towards us and asked if we had seen two strayed camels; though we could not help him to find them, we were able to tell him in which direction they had not wandered. Another half-hour and the silver-grey dots that are the iron roofs of the houses, and some green trees, came in sight. We whished down in front of the solid stone-built police station, whose doors opened hospitably, and Sergeant and Mrs. Stott came out to receive me. This brought the first part of the camel journey to an end, a distance of three hundred and twenty-five miles, which had taken me a fortnight to cover. The mailmen do it in twelve days.

# 3

## NEAR ALICE

*Weave o'er the world your weft, yea weave yourselves, Imperial races weave the warp thereof.* - W.M. Rossetti

AMONG the interesting places near Alice Springs are the Arltunga Gold Fields and the Hermannsberg Mission, near which grow some wonderful cycads and palms, remnants of a lost vegetation that has survived only in this particular spot. When I asked whether these particular trees and plants could not be cultivated in other districts I learnt that probably the position of the southern slopes of the Macdonnell Ranges is unique.

The Ranges are only two or three hundred feet high, but they rise abruptly from the plain, and look imposing. Mrs. Stott took me for a picnic to Simpson's Gap, a "black tracker" (native policeman) driving us through the Bush. All the horses were poor, shadowy things, and the state of all animals was truly pitiable. Most of the trees upon which cattle can feed had been cut down for them to demolish. At Simpson's Gap a little band of euros (small kangaroo) came hopping out towards us from the rocks, and turned off and vanished over the top of the range. The water in the Gap was black with dirt, and the animals had tried to make a soak for themselves before they would drink it.

With heads and hoofs they bored holes in the ground into which the water would sometimes filter, but many dry holes testified to their vain efforts. We came upon a tunnel about four feet long, with a little water at the end, which the tracker said a cow had scooped out with her horns.

All the waterholes were places of tragedy. At Emily Gap the water was shallow and black. Bush horses came down to drink, whinnied to the buggy horses in friendly fashion, and went to the water, but they did not seem able to touch it.

Dead horses and bullocks were lying at the edge, and cattle coming to the water would not pass them, but made a wide detour. A lovely mare and foal came down, saw the dead horses, shied, and rushed away. Presently they returned, found the water undrinkable, and went away again thirsty into the Bush.

The black tracker made a soak with his hands, and thus got some fairly clean water to fill the quart pots, and in spite of all the surrounding tragedies, we had a pleasant little picnic.

In a country where the conservation of water is of such vital importance, I was surprised to find no precautions at all taken to ensure its cleanliness. It appears to be nobody's business to see that carcases are burnt or buried. A dead dingo added to the dangers already existing. Dingoes are killed by means of poisoned baits, which take effect when they drink water. The Government of the Northern Territory pays 2s. 6d. a head for dingo scalps as compared to 7s. 6d. paid by the Government of South Australia. Consequently there is a brisk trade in " dogging," and many are the scalps taken in the Northern Territory and paid for in the South.

Sergeant Stott, who had lived for forty years in the Northern Territory, and whose advice was therefore of great assistance to me, arranged the next stage of my Journey.

It can be no easy task to hold the scales of justice in a sparsely populated slice of country about ten times the size of England when the claims of the retreating black man and the invading white man happen to clash, and clear-headedness and initiative characterize the Police Sergeant, whose authority has been all but absolute.

The laws are simple, and within the comprehension of the natives. They are based on the live-and-let-live principle, it being understood that the black man shall do no harm to the white man, his servants, or his property. There are still many natives who have not yet corne under the white man's influence - protective or otherwise - and with these the law does not concern itself, their affairs being settled by their own tribal law. They are therefore free to go their own way, even to the extent of eating their babies, without interference from their enlightened brothers.

Cattle-spearing, or robbery of any kind, is quickly put down, and the small gaol at Alice Springs receives the offender, after he has been dealt with by a Justice, who may be a telegraph operator or a station manager, but is always a responsible person, properly sworn in. Serious crimes necessitate a march to Darwin, some eight hundred miles away, the constable, locally called the "trooper," and escort travelling on horseback, the prisoners linked together, and footing it all the way at the rate of twenty-five miles a day.

There are some lonely spots. One white man rode into Alice Springs the other day remarking that he had not seen a white woman for four years.

Here, as in the north, the Springs are but a name.

The township is watered from the large artesian basin that underlies the district. Gardens flourish if irrigated twice a day, but fruit is scarce, a hasty Administrator some years ago having ordered the destruction of all citrus trees throughout the territory, because those at Darwin were attacked by some pest, Alice Springs, about eight hundred miles away, whose fruit-trees were in a healthy condition, not excepted.

The need for white women in the Northern Territory is proved by the relative numbers of white children and half-caste, for while there were only eight white children of school age, nearly forty little half-castes were being maintained in a refuge called the Bungalow at the Government's expense. Here, apparently, they looked after themselves. All slept in the same room at night, and the girls at the age of twelve and the boys at fourteen were drafted off into the service of anyone who had no prejudice against them. They seemed bright children. I saw them at work in the school, and was rather impressed by their neat writing, correct reading, and good memory.

Probably a resident doctor in Alice Springs would make life easier for parents of young families. I met a man there who had just bought a station some miles out, and intended to live there with his wife and eight children. He said that if the doctors in the south once visited the place, they would be quite willing to take up their abode there, for the interesting study that the natives afforded from a medical point of view.

There were thirty-six white people in Alice Springs, and they seemed a very united little community. The need of a church and a dispensary is probably felt either consciously or unconsciously by all. Across

Aboriginal children at the Bungalow, Alice Springs.

The Arunta camp near the Government Well, just outside the township of Alice Springs in 1924.

the road from the police station stood a partly built hostel of the Australian Inland Mission, which the Government intended to finish building and "equip" with two nurses. The dwellers in the Dead Heart have little recreation, but I was pleased to find a tennis club being opened, and enjoyed a good game on the opening day. The court was beautifully made of a substance called ant-bed, from the abandoned ants' nests in the neighbourhood, than which material there is nothing better for a hard court in a hot climate. One of the oldest inhabitants of the Alice Springs district, Mr. Bulingal, a traveller and prospector, who had taken the trouble to make minute notes of the country that had come under his observation, was kind enough to lend me these manuscripts so that I might get an idea of the district farther afield than I had time to travel.

Plans for the remainder of the journey were now practically settled. Sergeant Stott arranged for me to take Sir Sidney's plant as far as Tennant's Creek, beyond which point there would be no camel transport on account of the dangers of the ironwood tree.

The postal authorities in Adelaide, upon hearing that I was travelling north, kindly arranged to run a buggy from the Tennant to Powell's Creek, for which I was very grateful to them. Otherwise it would have been difficult to get enough horses for the baggage owing to the dry season. The stage from Powell's Creek to the Katherine River (about three hundred and seventy miles) remained doubtful for several days.

The letters in that district go by "contract mail," the mailman owning the plant and merely, as the terms suggests, contracting to carry the mails, and at liberty to take or decline a passenger as he chooses. We could not, however, get into touch with the mailman, communication being particularly difficult because the Katherine Races "were on," but the telegraph station master at the Katherine River telegraphed to Mr. Allchurch, at Stuart, near Alice Springs, that he thought it would be all right. . This verbal " all right" from a third, or rather from a fourth, party may seem slender assurance in view of the length and description of the journey I was about to undertake. But the experience that I had already had of the Bush showed me the hearty fashion in which travellers are assisted and sped on their way, and I had no intention of giving up the journey unless some calamity made it quite impossible to proceed. So I regarded the matter as comfortably arranged. And kindly messages came' over the telephone that the North would be pleased to meet me when I arrived, and would give me a welcome.

I was glad to continue with the same plant, for I felt that I understood these particular natives, and they had got used to me. All natives will not go beyond their own district, even when travelling with white people, for' the tribes look upon strangers with suspicion, especially when feed and water are scarce. But Tennant's Creek was Macumba Jack's own country, and Topsy had been part of the way, travelling with a camel-string, when she was a girl. The same language - Arunta - carried them all the way, and from time to time they met friends. There had been a touching encounter near Charlotte Waters, when Topsy and a lubra, who was walking along the distant horizon, suddenly espied each other, and the lubra flew to meet Topsy as the needle flies to the magnet.

Topsy presented her with a bundle of dirty old clothes - a gift of cryptic meaning - for to wash them would have been to deprive them of their essential virtue - the dear one's grime.

The boy was a good pilot, knew his work, and did it, but apart from this his intelligence was like that of a child. His idea of time and distance was very vague, and I sometimes asked him how far we had travelled just to hear what the reply would be, and he might say twelve miles or forty, showing that he neither understood the distance nor the time spent on the road. Nevertheless, he had an excellent memory for country. He was a good-looking native, with a stout though athletic figure, a straight back, and good-humoured face with high cheek bones, broad flat nose, curly black hair and beard and good brown eyes.

Topsy was much the same type, also stout and active, straight of figure (did anyone ever see an Aboriginal with a stoop ?), and small wrists and ankles.

Everybody was looking forward to rain, but I do not think anybody expected it. Alice Springs has a rainfall of $11^{1/2}$ inches, which generally falls between November and February. Oodnadatta has only $6^{1/2}$ inches per annum, but that country is so fertile that even 2 inches of rain followed a few days later by a quarter of an inch will give an excellent season. I think this is chiefly due to a friendly little Michaelmas daisy that springs up among the gibbah and flowers profusely, yielding an excellent feed for stock.

Experiments in cereal growing have been disappointing, for the grain matures before it is fully grown, but I fully believe that if the inhabitants would only persevere with these experiments year after year, a seed-wheat or seed-oat would be "bred" that would stand the climate. Some useful result would surely come in time. The plains that lie among the stone country look so extraordinarily fertile that it seems a sad pity for them to be lying uncultivated.

The day before I left Alice Springs Macumba Jack came to my door remarking casually that Ladybone was ill. Enquiries elucidated that she was not "sick," but "hollow," accompanied by that expressive upward jerk of thumbs under ribs, by which a native intimates short rations. He said that he had not been able to find any feed for the animals, though he had taken them farther and farther into the Bush every day. I told him to go out with a tomahawk and cut down branches, and he said that he would cut down "six trees."

I bade good-bye to Sergeant Stott and his capable wife, who had taken so much trouble on my behalf, mounted my camel, and rode out under the gateway. I stopped at the telegraph station at Stuart, about two miles away, to say farewell to the Allchurch family, who gave me a very hearty send-off. My last sight of them was a hat waved aloft on a stick as I made my way among the rocks. The camels seemed very tired and weakly, and on coming to a beautiful gidgea tree in full bloom we cut it down relentlessly, and they devoured every blossom. The country was so badly eaten out that even a camel found it hard to pick up a living.

All day we wound about among the rocks of the Macdonnell Ranges through desolate-looking country that was given up to stunted shrubs and henbane. A white man with a mob of horses passed while I was at dinner on his way to Bond Springs, one of Sir Sidney Kidman's stations, managed by Mr. Draper, a retired soldier. He said he had travelled up from Oodnadatta three days behind me, with a string of camels.

About four o'clock we reached the flat country, and the Macdonnell Ranges were a thing of the past. I halted for a meal just short of the Sixteen-mile Creek, and then rode on again until half-past nine, having done twenty-five miles. Unfortunately, we camped just short of a good feed, so that the camels went a long way back in search of " tucker," and it was late

Bond Springs Station.

Sergeant Robert Stott, in Alice Springs from 1911 to his death in 1928.

before they were brought in the next morning. It was a cold night, with a cloudy sky, and rain looked imminent. When I arose at five I thought we were in for a wet day, and prepared accordingly, but the clouds blew over and the sun became scorchingly hot. We put up three kangaroo, which the boy stalked, and came back saying he had hit "the ole man." The little bare trees were crowded with galah parrots, lovely birds with plumage of the softest pink and grey. They had seen us some distance off, and were screaming and clamouring in anticipation of a drink from the well. Macumba Jack loosed off his gun into the midst of these confiding little things, and got eight with one shot. It was a long day's travelling, owing to various delays, and we only accomplished twenty-one miles. The baggage camel became very sorry for herself, and began "singing out." We had to camp again in scrub country, where the feed is never very good, and where the camels take a good deal of looking for in the morning. After we had made camp there were various duties. It was found necessary to cook the meat that night in order to keep it, etc.

As we got nearer to the Poison Belt I began to get a little anxious about the future, for I had not yet decided upon any definite course of action. There were two ways of proceeding, firstly by tying up the camels at night, and feeding them with cut branches, when they would be safe only as long as they were tied, and in imminent danger later, for when released hungry they would eat the first greenstuff they saw, which might happen to be gastrolobium or indigo bush; or they must be left to feed as usual on the chance of coming upon the poison at any time. The boy was so long in bringing in the camels that morning that I began to wonder whether the poison bush had not made its way further south than is recorded. And then I remembered having seen him going off under the stars with his gun under his arm, and the camel cords in his hand, and I hoped that he was hunting. When the stars paled the birds began to sing. There is a common little bird that wakes the morning, faces the heat of noon with a song, and sings the sun to sleep. I have never seen him. The natives call him hevalaval, and told me that he was "all same wren," but this only meant that he was a small brown bird. Then a wagtail flitted into a mulga bush, sluing his tail to left and right, not up and down in the English mode. The hour of dawn is always interesting in the Bush, particularly when one has camped in the dark the night before. The place that I had slept in, but never seen, now came into view: mulga scrub on all sides somewhat thick, clumps of white" silver-grass," and very many ancient ant-hills rising like terra-cotta tombstones.

I hoped to reach Connor's Well by eight, but it was not to be. There was a two-hours' wait for the camels. Presently the boy came into view, leading the string. "Been a long way," he said in answer to enquiries, and sat down to have his breakfast. You cannot hurry a native, nor a camel, and you cannot retard the sun's progress at morn and evening and hurry him through the heat of the day, which I should dearly like to have done. I wished I had thought of providing myself with a camel bell before starting, for I feared that if I had many more experiences like this I might "miss the bus" at Tennant's Creek.

At Connor's Well two natives were drawing water with a "whip," and a big mixed mob of animals was crowding and panicking by turns round the short trough. Poor thirsty beasts, with their eyes nearly dropping out of their heads, would just get a mouthful of water, and then be pushed aside on to the edge of the crowd, and have to wait their turn again, queue-fashion. A great raw-boned draught horse kicked mightily, letting fly to right and left, making it known that he was going to have a satisfactory drink before all the water was gone, and a little thin mare, who had several times essayed to get to the water, lost her foal in a sudden scatter, and the tiny thing went about questing for her. Cows and calves, nearly dropping with weakness, tried to find a place at the trough, but they only seemed to get a mouthful before they were pushed away. Then a big spent bull, in such poor condition that he was hardly able to walk, took a few steps forward and rested, bellowed to the others to make room for him, walked on a little farther, and stood helpless, and then pawed the ground as if impatient at his own weakness.

While the camels were drinking the boy surprised me by reporting a mob of motor-cars on the road. I could see nothing, but presently some little dots came into sight, and he discovered that they were not motor-cars, but horses, and" one white man, two black fellah."

The white man was the one who had passed me near Stuart.

"You do travel," he said. "I camped three miles behind you last night. You have done already pretty well this morning, and shot a turkey on the way. I saw the tracks."

I told him about the disappointing start, but he was too busy commenting on the pace I was travelling to show any sympathy. "You will get to Ryan's Well to-night," he said. "Only nineteen miles from here. I am coming that way, so I shall see you later."

Almost as soon as we had left him the big tin basin fell off the top of the load, and away went Barley at a canter, pulling the poor baggage camel along after her, so fast that she got a sore nose in the process. The other two also "got the hump" promptly, and everything was in commotion. The load had tipped sideways, so we had to whish down, unload, and load up again. The affair took over half an hour, and I was afraid that the man whom we had left at the well would pass by before I had got things tidied up, and would alter his opinion about my being a fast traveller. But as a matter of fact he did not catch us up at all, and I never saw him again. The blacks were disappointed when I told them that, owing to the delay, we must have a short dinner camp, and that they would not be able to cook their turkey until the evening.

Mr. and Mrs. Nicker of Glen Maggie, at Ryan's Well, easily persuaded me to stay the night, and I heard a good deal from them of the difficulties and disappointments of the people who live in the Dead Heart. At Glen Maggie it was the lambing season, and though there was good salt bush and cotton bush growing six miles from the well, it was too far for the sheep to travel to them, and it was impossible to get food cut and brought to the sheep.

The evening's conversation was thoroughly interesting, and would have been very enjoyable also had it not been that during this exceptionally dry season the sufferings of the animals and the consesequent difficulties and privations of the settlers are very affecting.

My boy and lubra vanished suddenly over the horizon, taking the camels with them, and the next morning it transpired that they had fled from infection, there being an outbreak of influenza, which is often fatal to natives, among the blacks at Glen Maggie.

Eugene Nicker, the youngest son, had lately done a long camel ride alone, with only one camel, and said that he had managed quite comfortably by tying up his mount at night, and feeding it with branches

It is, of course, too risky for a solitary traveller to let his animal loose to graze, in case he should not find it again.

I listened to all advice as I went upon my way, and reflected upon it in camp in the evening. It certainly was a good idea to tie up the camels, hobbling them as loosely as possible, and fastening the tether to the hobble chain.

I sometimes repeated Mr. Walter Duncan's advice to make for the O.T. if I got into any real difficulty, but though I had thought this humorous, it was always received with seriousness, the answer generally being: "Many a poor fellow perishing for water has done it, and sometimes the telegraph people have got to him in time, and sometimes they haven't."

On one occasion a half-caste boy, walking along, tossed a bit of wire over the line, which broke the current, and gave him an electric shock in the arm. "He cheeky fellah. He bite," said the half-caste. He tried to pull off the wire, received another shock, so let it be.

As he travelled along he met a lineman driving out from the telegraph station to look for the damage, who asked him, "What's the matter with the line?"

"He cheeky fellah. He bite," said the half-caste, fingering his arm. So the lineman knew who had caused the trouble. He invited the half-caste to go with him to Alice Springs, but the boy declined. The lineman insisted. "Come and do a walk-about," he said. The unfortunate boy set out, thinking the expedition was going to be a picnic. When they reached Alice Springs, however, he was sent to gaol for three months for tampering with the overland telegraph.

One day the boy shot a kangaroo, which we all helped to stalk, for while he dismounted and went after it with his gun, Topsy and I attracted its atten¬tion towards the camels, and it was so busy watching us that it let the boy get within easy range. I felt very sad when it proved to be a female with a young one in her pouch. The only thing to do was to knock it on the head with a gun butt immediately. Be it said here that the old Bush belief concerning the marsupial birth dies hard. One intelligent white woman whom I met declared that she had witnessed the supposed phenomena with her own eyes.

The natives cooked the kangaroo in the traditional way. They dug a hole in the ground, lined it with hot embers and earth, put in the kangaroo in its skin, and then covered up the whole thing with embers and earth and lighted branches.

I offered Macumba Jack five shillings for the skin of the kangaroo, which he declined on the score that if he skinned the kangaroo, he would have to boil it, and that a boiled kangaroo had not the flavour of a roasted one. During the night we had the excitement of a snake hunt, and the boy was very uneasy, because he had said he had found a snake just on the spot where Barley had been rolling, and he was afraid she might have been bitten. Topsy and I kept up an illumination by throwing tufts of lighted grass while the boy killed it.

What with the snake hunt and the kangaroo orgy, it was a disturbed night, and I found it difficult to arouse my retainers in the morning.

The homestead at Ryan Well as remembered b y Margaret Knickers.

# 4

*The Long Trail, The trail that is always new.*

- KIPLING

THE next day we reached Ti-tree Well, and found Mr. Heffanan and Mr. Ambrose just returning from branding. I was a surprise to them, for they had not known that I was on the way.

Mr. Ambrose had brought a mob of cattle through the poison zone with less disaster than has attended any other drover, and I was an interested listener to his account of it, when we heard sounds of excitement outside.

"It's those camels," said Mr. Heffanan, and we beheld the tucker-box turning a somersault in the air and pouring out its contents. The camel-boxes had been tossed off, the riding camels were off into the Bush as fast as they could gallop, and the two that were linked together, rein to crupper, were solemnly executing a *pas de deux*. The white men were most kind and helpful. One shouted to a servant, "Saddle a horse in case I have to ride after the camels," and the other collected, dusted, and repacked the scattered property. The boy got the camels back before they had gone very far, which was fortunate, for a runaway camel sometimes means a whole day lost, and I was told that 'Usshan' Khan, the Alice Springs mailman, had to chase one of his for five-and-twenty miles after a stampede.

We loaded up again, and nothing was the worse for the mishap. The whole commotion was caused by two small kids, which strolled out of the goat-yard to have a look at the camels.

I camped a few miles farther on, beside the telegraph line, and the next day reached Central Mount Stuart (or Sturt).

The day was scorchingly hot. I had intended to climb the Mount, see as much of Australia as was visible from this central spot, and fill in, as I gazed upon the prospect, as much of her history and geography as I could recall. So far history and geography have gone hand in hand in Australia, for it is the geographers who have chiefly made the history.

My resolution failed me, however, for I did not feel inclined to face the heat and the effort. Topsy brought me a pannikin of water out of

Bullocky Soak, and I did what I have often tried to prevent others from doing - drank it without looking at it. My disgust was great when I glanced at the dregs and saw that the water was filmy and filthy and altogether detestable, and I determined that if I escaped the consequences that I richly deserved for this piece of carelessness, I would refrain from drinking dirty water again! The creek at Bullocky Soak was parching and shelterless, and there were mirage effects everywhere. The boy did his best for my comfort, and cut down two or three little trees to make a shelter, but as there were not any leaves on them it was not of much avail.

There were thousands of diamond sparrows, whose activities I found very diverting, but the place was so arid that I was glad to be on the move again, for the saddle was cooler than the parching ground.

A few miles farther on we arrived unexpectedly at very pretty country. After crossing a large claypan we toiled up a ridge of sandhills, and came upon a really beautiful and extensive view of the Stirling country, miles of mulga scrub in the blue distance giving a very unusual softness to the landscape.

Hanson's Well was as bare a place as I had yet seen. The only living thing in sight was a poor horse hanging round the empty water trough in the hopes that someone would turn up to draw a bucket of water for him before he perished. The water from the well was very bad, but the camels did not object to it, and after we had left I saw the poor old horse making his painful way towards the well. I think it was his last drink. I have seen many sad sights. Sometimes very far from water or feed we passed a few cattle standing with lowered heads. They did not move off at the approach of the camels. Often they did not even turn their heads, but sometimes they would look at me, or so I thought, with *Ora pro nobis* in their eyes. Of course, they were doomed. To-morrow their heads would be lower. Then they would sink down. I saw them in every stage.

Mr. Alec Ross at Stirling Station told me something about the early days in the Central Mount Stuart district. Apparently the country was more settled than it is at present, and one hopes that when the railway comes it will do all that is expected of it.

For several miles a little party of Bush camels had been following us, and we could not shake them off. At the Stirling homestead Mr. Ross yarded them, for he said that though they appeared to be harmless, they might stampede my camels in the night, and as I am not fond of night alarms, I was grateful to him.

I had been expecting to meet an Afghan called Allah Mahomed (Mahomet Allum), coming south with a camel string, who would give me information about the poisons.

One evening we heard camel bells about a mile to the north, and early in the morning I walked out to find his camp.

He greeted me with the dignified "Salaam, memsahib," of his country, followed by an Australian handshake. He had only lost two camels out of a string of sixty-three, and one of them had died of old age, and the other had wandered into the Bush to calve, and would probably return to the string later.

He told me that it would be unwise to tie up the camels at night and feed them with branches as I had meant to do, but advised grazing them in the ordinary way, hurrying over stony places and "gaps" where the weed was thickest, and halting beside the ashes of his own camp-fires, as these stopping-places had proved to be safe ones. He said that the stony country was the only danger.

He willingly produced a camel bell, saying, "I give you, I give you."

"What shall I give you?" I asked.

"No, no. I give *you*."

"Thank you very much," said I. "Do you eat chutney?"

"I eat chutney," he replied. So I reciprocated with some chutney and barley sugar.

These big strings of camels only travel about fifteen miles a day, because they have the cow camels and their calves with them. They seldom start until ten in the morning. The camels are allowed to go their natural pace, which is two and a half miles an hour, so that it is no tax upon them. It is a pretty sight to see the calves gambolling beside their mothers.

Barrow Creek telegraph station is a historic spot owing to the native attack on the place in 1873, when the station master and blacksmith were both murdered. Their graves lie in a little enclosure near the compound, and though history does not record that their death has been avenged, a creek called Skull Creek, about half a mile away, might tell a different tale.

"Whished down."

Mahomet Allum, Afghan cameleer and herbalist of the Bush.

The officers to-day have more peaceful lives. Mr. Lawson and Mr. Welburn received me very hospitably, entertained me to dinner, and sped me on my way with fresh food and kind wishes. A mixture of climate and skill enabled them to grow tomatoes all the year round.

"Camp near the shackle, this side of the jump-up," they advised, "then you will get a good night, with no fear of poison weed"; and then jocularly, "Knock off an insulator if you want any help, and we will come along."

I replied that I knew there was a heavy penalty for interfering with the overland telegraph.

"So there is," they answered, "but we would say the parrots did it."

That evening I met with the sage-bush that I had believed to be a camel poison. To say that we camped warily gives a poor idea of the extreme caution with which Macumba Jack and I led along two of the camels, Topsy holding the other two, and gingerly allowed them to graze. We held them on very short strings, ready to pull the weed out of their mouths if necessary. When we found that they did not touch the sage-bush, but nosed in and out among it, eating other weeds, we hobbled them and let them go as usual.

I was soon, however, to see the effect of noxious weeds upon cattle. Near Taylor's Well we came upon the carcases of about fifteen hundred poisoned beasts that the crows would not touch, lying in twos and threes, and sometimes in heaps. We could hardly get the camels to go forward. I can give no idea of the sinister effect of the bright sunshine and foul atmosphere, nor can I describe the feeling of loneliness that came over me when I found myself in the midst of the devastation, riding along with compressed lips, reins tied to saddle, a stout mulga switch in each hand, working with these and my heels to urge my unwilling camel on. It was a relief to reach clean country and get into camp, which we did a little way north of Limestone Hill.

The next watering-place was at Wydiffe Well, which remote spot has been the home of Mrs. Crooke and her husband and daughters for many years. Their nearest women neighbour in the south was Mrs. Nicker, a hundred and twenty-five miles away, and to the north a family named Bohning, one hundred and eighty-five miles away. One of the daughters told me that when the Bohning family passed their home with a mob of cattle and goats a few months before, she had not seen a white woman for three and a half years. They entertained me very kindly to dinner, and the girls were so prettily dressed that one would not have imagined they led such an isolated life. I parted from Mrs. Crooke with real regret that I could not make a longer stay. Among those women who face life in the wilds and separation from the society of friends I thought Mrs. Crooke was the bravest.

The indigo bush and sage bush that wrought such havoc among the cattle do no harm to camels. My real anxiety began when we reached the big round rocks called Devil's Marbles, where the gastrolobium is rife. This shrub, with its tender green leaf and blossom rather like a wallflower, has invited many a camel to death. So far no certain cure has been found, but one man is supposed to have been saved his animals with a dose of Condy's Crystals. Needless to say, I kept this handy, but luckily had no need to use it. Macumba Jack proved himself a good pilot. He walked on ahead, weeding the gastrolobium from the path and threw it aside. The camels were "tied short," nose-cord to crupper, so that they could not stretch their long necks out very far. Under the shadow of a Marble a solitary pedestrian was boiling himself a billy-can of tea. He said that in another two hours we should be out of the danger zone, and added, "but over there, two miles to the eastward, a friend of mine lost fifteen of his thirty camels in a night." He was Mr. McHugh on his way to Wycliffe Well, "foot-walking."

By this time Topsy was so tired of camel-riding that she could do no work in camp, but mooned about restlessly, looking for widgidees (edible caterpillars), of which the larger sort is dug out of tree-trunks with the aid of a hairpin lent by Aracucha, then lightly cooked in the embers, while the smaller sort is eaten *au naturel*. Next morning, when all should have been easy and the Poison ⊠one a thing of the past, the lead camel suddenly began to "sing out," lay down and rolled. The boy did not wish me to try the remedy.

"Might be hungry, might be tired. Mulga over there," he said.

We loaded her with the baggage to discourage further rolling, and rushed the string along to the mulga, and all four camels were soon feeding contentedly, but if Barley had wanted to make my flesh creep, she could have found no surer way of doing it.

The Bonny Well was a rickety construction, much eaten by white ants. I had doubts whether the rotten framework would stand the strain of hauling up a heavy bucket of water. I should have felt very disconcerted if I had broken the well so that travellers coming after me could not have got water! Fortunately there was no mishap.

My friends at Barrow Creek had warned me not to camp within two miles of Kelly Well, because big black ants, of the kind that bite, had taken up a four-mile block in that locality and populated it densely. I was for camping on the hither side, but the boy pointed out that there was no feed here at all, so we persevered until the dark silhouette of Kelly Well appeared before us. Something was wrong with the tackle here also, and by the time the boy had got it rigged, darkness had fallen. Topsy was so tired and seedy that I did not think it would be safe for her to climb the rickety ladder, so when the boy called, "Want someone, please," I went up myself. He only needed a third hand to steady the winder while he tipped up the bucket, but the yawning abyss of the well, the darkness, the spring-back of the winder, and my own fatigue made the filling of the canteens an uncertain business. It was no use camping in the domain of the black ants, so we pilgrimaged still farther in order to get beyond the two-mile limit. The camels stamped their feet and began dancing about when the ants bit them. Finally, after searching the ground with lights, we found a place that seemed clean enough to camp, and I for one felt glad when the day's march was over.

In the morning, though the boy had made an early start to fetch the camels, it was long ere he arrived, and even at 8.30 there was no sign of him. Dawn showed us open country, red earth, and a low scrub. As time went on Topsy kept on going out to look for him and coming back. She was afraid that he had had an accident, and I was afraid that he had found all the camels dead or dying. It was no good trying to follow him, for we did not know what direction he had gone. Of course, the thought that suggested itself was that there must have been unknown poison growing off the track. I reflected that we were only three miles from water at Kelly Well, and only thirty-two miles from Tennant's Creek telegraph station, also that the mail should pass this way in five days, and we had enough food to hold out till then. I was in the frame of mind when one still hopes for the best, though one prepares for the worst, when at ten o'clock a tired black fellah, sitting on the hump of the first of four camels, came slowly into camp. He said they went ten miles, which means that he must have gone about twenty miles. He had been absent for five hours, having done half a day's work before the day's work began.

He sat down to his breakfast with a resigned air, while Topsy loaded up. The camels had evidently stampeded, for all had broken their hobble straps, and I suppose they had passed all the way through the black ants' territory without having had any rest or feed during the night. For myself, I had awakened with a headache, so strange an occurrence that I searched my memory for any possible cause, and presently remembered that during the varied incidents of the preceding day, while I was trying to identify a new bird by means of Mr. Leach's "Bird Book," my eyes on the page instead of on the road, the Oont had suddenly rushed off into the Bush, and carried me under the low branch of a tree; and it was well for me that I was wearing a pith hat (though, of course, it was rather bad for the pith hat).

I was able, however, to kill a snake, which was sitting beside me at breakfast-time, tied in a very ornamental knot closely resembling a piece of the root of the tree which sheltered him, and only distinguishable from it because he overdid his part, and was more like the root of a tree than the root itself was. He was a death adder, with a wedge on the end of his tail that made him a scorpion as well as a snake, for he threw it over his back and stabbed as well as bit. He tried it on the stick I used to kill him with, and I was able to watch all his manoeuvres.

My little party had conscientiously observed Sergeant Stott's instructions to put out the camp-fire before moving on; but ahead of us we saw the smoke of five different Bush fires, which probably had their origin in smoke-signals, the native method of sending news through the Bush. No white man has yet solved the mystery of the native "wireless," and the extraordinary way in which natives, isolated from their fellows, are able to receive news of them. Many people think this must be due to telepathy, because smoke could not bring news in detail. This, of course, was quite diff-

Mr. McHugh, "the foot-walker" at the Devil's Marbles.

The Tennant Creek Telegraph Station.

of course, was quite different from the mulga wire gossip that entertains, with its extravagant scandals, the white people who are linked together by the telephone. I was told it would shock me if I could have heard the flights of fancy to which the gossips attain. But it supplies the want of an evening paper, and assures at least some people having a cheery hour, and probably does more good than harm.

We were in no danger from the Bush fires, because they had already crossed our path, but a north wind, which continued for two days to cover us with dust and nearly suffocate us with smoke, was rather trying; also the heat was intense.

After the quiet of the Bush, Tennant's Creek seemed bustlingly active. Besides the telegraph station master, Mr. Rabbitt, and his assistant, who gave me a very kind reception, the line party had come in for their stores, making a total of six white men.

The line party travels beside the Overland Telegraph at the rate of five miles a day, keeping it in repair, and cutting away the Bush. An important part of their work is the tautening of the two wires after a few hundred parrots have perched upon them and suddenly taken flight. I heard again that the last resource of an overlander, who falls sick or cannot get to water, is to make for the telegraph line and damage it, certain that the slightest interruption to messages will bring repairing parties from the nearest stations, and though such interference is punishable by law, people have been known to take the risk in the hope that indulgent telegraph officers will report that the damage was done by parrots. I had a feeling for the line, having day after day watched the short metal poles coming rhythmically to meet me at the rate of one a minute, by which I could gauge the camel's pace at three miles an hour.

Most of the natives at the Tennant had gone off to do a "walk-about," but a number of lubras were encamped in the creek, all of whom refused to speak because the men had "put a silence on them." It was entertaining to watch the weekly issue of rations to women who would not utter a word, asked for tea and sugar in pantomime, and grunted approval. Evidently it was not the first time they had been under the ban, for their gestures were unanimous. A sprinkling movement of the hand indicated sugar, and the gesture of taking up a pinch of something and dropping it into an unseen billy-can was sufficient indication that they wished for tea. They were all simply clad in men's shirts, and the one who wore a battered old hat did so with the air of" painting the lily."

Some of them had strange names; one stalwart lubra, evidently a person of importance, answered to the name of Dying Duck.

Farther north I came upon natives who had had a silence put upon them as a sign of mourning.

Macumba Jack belonged to this tribe, so he took up his abode in their camp, but by tribal custom, Topsy, who was a native of Aldnagowra, near Oodnadatta, was not admitted, so she spent her time sitting on the doorstep of my room, getting my things ready for the next stage of the journey, and regaling me with gossip about the other lubras and the strenuous ordeal which a young boy was undergoing during his initiation into manhood - how every evening he was "killed" with a stick, etc.

The dust storms and the smoke resulted in my losing my voice, and for the first day after my arrival Mr. Rabbitt had practically a dumb visitor. Some of the line party played bridge, and we enjoyed a rubber or two in the post office, our kindly host busy at his desk the while, and a tiny foal that had been knocked into the water trough during a stampede of cattle, and rescued by the line party, came and looked on. This was the most confiding little animal imaginable, though it had evidently inherited buck-jumping instincts, for one touch of a finger would make it draw its hoofs together and hump its back. Its mother was lost, and it remained at the telegraph station until a mob of horses came in one evening for water, and the line party foisted it off on another mare, and hoped they had been successful. I now saw the first flowers in bloom since I left Adelaide, with the exception of the henbane, wild fuchsia, and a few other Bush varieties. Before the door of the telegraph station grew two very fine oleander bushes, each a mass of blossom, giving the place the air of an oasis.

The pack-horse mail arrived from the south in charge of Mailman Sam Lynch, who had ridden thirty-seven thousand miles during his seven years' service without ever being late or losing a parcel With him came Mr. Phillips, the new station master for Powell's Creek, one hundred and twenty miles north, who had never been in the saddle until he left Oodnadatta on the seven hundred and seventy mile ride to take up his new duties.

# 5

*The Treasure of Patriotism In Lands remote.*
  - W.M. ROSSETTI

I NOW sent the plant so kindly lent me by Sir Sidney Kidman back to the Macumba station. It had brought me along safely for six hundred and fifty miles. Topsy reiterated her little farewell "Goo'bye, I lose you. I lonely." Both she and the boy proved trustworthy and efficient, and I think that they were particularly good types of their race. I arranged that on their return journey the boy and lubra should be provided with food and money when they were half-way home, which seemed a necessary precaution in view of their socialistic instincts and gambling tendencies, for I am sure that they would have shared their last crust with their fellows as readily as they would have gambled away their only coat; but it was not reassuring to be told by a man who knew the natives well that they would probably arrive at their own station quite destitute.

"They won't have a rag to wear nor a penny to spend nor a mouthful of food," he said, "but they are always like that. The people at the stations will look after them, for we all know that they go back to their wild state the moment they leave a white master or mistress."

I could not have believed this of Macumba Jack and Topsy, and I often wondered if it were the case, but I never heard in what state they arrived.

The night before we started the man who had been overhauling the buggy sought me out and advised me to keep on the camels and continue the journey with them because, he said, though he had put two days' work into the buggy, he was still afraid that the wheels would "turn inside out"; he also remarked we were starting off with thirteen horses. It would have been dangerous, however, to take the camels among the ironwood, apart from the fact that they might be needed at their own station, so I decided to take the buggy and trust my luck; and it carried us through quite safely, though we were not without moments of anxiety about it.

I said good-bye to my kind and courteous host who, with his colleagues, had made the few days' halt both pleasant and interesting, and took my seat beside the driver. We stopped at midday at a tiny copse called Sam's Trees, which the mailman said was a "lovely little dinner shade."

We watered the horses that afternoon at the Carryman Lagoon (which seemed to be chiefly mud), and had a dry camp that night at Gibson's Creek, choosing a bit of hard ground to avoid snakes. My camp was pitched beside the buggy, and the black boy, who rode in charge of the eleven spare horses, made me a bed of fragrant gum leaves that was softer than any mattress. The horses did not get a drink until next morning, when, after crossing the South Hayward, Middle Hayward, and North Hayward, all of which were dry, we found water in the Attack Creek, which holds out longer than most, being fed from the Short and Wittington Ranges. It was here that Stuart, the explorer, had a historic fight with the natives, making his way through the Attack Gap as far as the Creek, where he was driven back, and my companions now told me that he suffered so heavily that he had to return to Adelaide for reinforcements.

I felt truly sorry for our animals; the second pair of horses could hardly do any work, and one of them had to be left behind to be picked up later when the mail returned. The next pair were in little better case. They stood still and endured a very futile flogging, apparently unable to move, and it was only when the men put their shoulders to the wheels that the poor, half-starved creatures could start.

The native grasses of the different localities - porcupine, spinifex, Mitchell, bogobine - had now given place to a variety that the mailman called water grass, reddish stalks, with no description of blade, but which the horses seemed to enjoy, though it looked anything but appetizing.

We passed Morphett Creek, and crossed the plain to Banka Banka, the station of the Ambrose brothers, whose courtesy and hospitality knew no bounds. The talk turned chiefly upon beef, cattle-raising in general, prospects and prices and the immediate need of a railway. "It's only when we get the railway that we shall be able to have our women with us," they said.

There were comfortable reclining-chairs, made of strips of bullocks' hide, and beds of the same interlaced material. Owing to our late arrival and early departure I did not see much of the station. I had heard that, in spite of the difficulties of the climate, Mr. Ambrose had a good garden, and the excellent meal prepared for us testified as much to the skill of the gardener as to that of the cook.

The buggy held out pretty well (the tires had been padded with greenhide), but it needed a little attention with a hammer from time to time. Also a bolt, fastening the swingle bar to the front carriage, jolted out, and the whole concern began to sway and rattle, and the pole to swing against the horse's legs in rather an alarming manner. The boy was sent to search beneath the telegraph line for a piece of discarded wire, and as he was fortunate in finding one the repair was quickly done.

At one point we overtook a travelling blacksmith encamped by the roadside, journeying alone with a buggy and two horses. He had come from Queensland, and was looking for work in the Northern Territory.

The Central Australian horse does not know the look of a water-bucket. He is always unharnessed and sent to the water. Our buggy horses could have had a drink here, for which they would have been grateful, if we had carried a bucket and if they were used to drinking out of it. But such a thing is never used. They had to pass the water-hole - which they did very regretfully - because there was not time to take them out. Happily they were sure of getting a drink at the end of the day.

We passed Wildguard Creek, Mucadi, Prentice's Lagoon (dry), the North and South Tonkinsons (also dry), and on to Helen Springs. About six miles before we reached the homestead the five Bohning children, who were all born in the Northern Territory, came cantering out to meet us. It was eleven days since I had seen a white woman, and Mrs. Bohning gave me a kindly welcome. There is a very interesting garden here, where various experiments were being tried, and Cape gooseberries, peanuts, and a pleasant-flavoured fruit called the Austral berry were successfully grown. They also had large flocks of goats, which are a great feature of life in the north. They are kept literally by the thousand, and thrive where cattle would starve. Mrs. Bohning told me that she had tried the experiment of giving a goat a sprig of gastrolobium to eat, and the animal instantly fainted, but recovered after a teaspoonful of Condy's Crystals had been poured down its throat.

The Bohning family run their station without any black labour. Both the boys and girls are very much at home on horseback, helping in the work of droving, cattle mustering, etc. They showed me an orphaned camel two years old that had been brought up by a goat which grew so attached to it that though she had had two sets of kids since she adopted it, she neglected them in its favour. The camel was so fond of its young master and so jealous of anyone who presumed to come near him that he inflicted a severe bite upon a tired young man who arrived at the station, and threw himself down to rest under the shelter of a tree where Jack Bohning sometimes lay.

One of the drawbacks to life in the north is the limitation of the parcel post to three pounds weight. I heard how one boot arrived alone, and its fellow was delivered by the next mail six weeks later; of a saddle forwarded in three-pound parcels to be re-made by the purchaser; of sheets and dress-lengths cut to fit the exigencies of the parcel post.

Part of the mailman's work is to keep an eye on the telegraph line and report if he sees anything wrong. He can do simple repairs, such as putting on a new insulator, and takes a repairing outfit with him. He told me of the difficulty of travelling in the "wet," one district, called the Gluepot, having a particularly bad reputation for bogging horses unawares.

The telegraph people at Powell's Creek were a cheery party, and entertained me most kindly. They told me they lived in the "snakiest" place in all Australia. Two "cheeky" ones were killed while I was there, and beside my door hung an arrangement of twisted wire called a "convincer," as a handy weapon. I witnessed a cattle muster a few miles away when Mr. Jarratt, the master, handed over to his successor, and we rode to the yard at a place called the Spring, and counted the cattle as they ran out. I believe that this Spring is the only one really worthy of the name that I had yet seen; there actually was a tiny trickle of running water, and even the tiniest trickle on the move makes a place beautiful. There were turpentine trees, paper bark gums, river gums, and some little birds called Winter-Jacks. A quart pot of tea quickly boiled on a little pile of sticks, and we returned to the station just as it was getting dark.

Mr. and Mrs. Bohning had arrived, bringing a horse that was to travel to Darwin by the mail. I found her conversation about matters connected with native life of the greatest interest. The Womra and the Lepi tribes of this district have not yet forsaken their cannibal habits, the old men, as usual, being the worst offenders in this direction. The Womra are baby-eaters, but it would seem as if they had an uneasy conscience in the matter, for they knock out two of their front teeth when they first begin this horrible custom, to let the child's spirit escape lest it should haunt them. They have many children, but the husband will only let the lubra keep two, the firstborn is always killed at birth, because the mother, who is generally about fourteen years old, is considered too young to bring it up. A few years ago, in the Powell's Creek district, there was a Massacre of Innocents; the young men, tired of taking their elder brothers' cast-off wives, and the young women tired of being married to old men, took the law into their own hands, and ran away together, so that the old people were left to starve. The elder men of the tribe (who rule the women absolutely) decreed that the male babies should die. An "old" man of perhaps forty will take all the daughters of a family and "grow" them (bring them up), and he has them as wives, passing them on in turn to his younger brother.

A white woman told me a very harrowing story of a lubra in her employ who went back to her husband's camp on a holiday with her child, aged about four years, which she was trying to bring up with particular care under her mistress's guidance. She went out hunting in the traditional fashion for her husband's food, and on her return the child was nowhere to be found. The woman in whose care it had been left could only shake her head, and would not utter a word. When pressed for a reply she had to own that in the mother's absence the child's father and his fellows had taken the child from her, and cooked and eaten it. The poor mother returned to her mistress in a state of grief and disappointment, which was rendered more pathetic by the fact that she could speak a little English, and told her the story brokenly, ending with, "You should 'a heard me cry."

There were so many people at Powell's Creek, what with the Bohning couple, the northern mailman and southern mailman, the two telegraph masters, the lineman, two men who were camped in the Creek, and myself, that it was supposed that there had never been so many white people there before. The evening passed cheerily. We made a four at bridge, and the rubber was accompanied by the running extravaganza of a man sitting near, so that the players had perforce to lower their hands and smile, remarking meanwhile, "Isn't Charlie a circus?" The wit of the party, however, was Mr. Sidney Smith. I do not know if he is any relation to his celebrated name-

Newcastle Waters Station.

The Katherine River Mail.

sake, but his conversation has the same sort of spice, the gift of humour being doubly valuable in the " snakiest" place in Australia. The two snakes that had both been killed while twisting up waggon wheels were skinned, cured with a mixture of soda and baking powder, and given to me as mementoes.

I was prepared to start the next morning with Mailman MacGregor on the three-hundred-mile journey to the Katherine River, doing the first sixty miles on horseback, for it had been impossible for the mailman to bring his buggy south of Newcastle Waters. Just as I was setting out, however, the Government contractor, Mr. Peacock, who was sinking a well in those parts, telephoned to say he was sending a car over the next day, and would be glad if I would make use of it. I had intended to do the whole journey in a leisurely fashion that would allow me to make observations of bird life, etc., on the way, but Mr. Peacock's kind offer was not to be declined, so the sixty miles to Newcastle Waters, which would have taken two days with the mail, was accomplished in a few hours.

The Bush changed slightly from time to time; ironwood, beefwood, lancewood, Bohemia tree, bullwaddy, and turpentine flanked the road. At South Newcastle, about midday, some brolgas or native companions and spoonbills were fishing in the milky pond. They ignored the arrival of a car, but took a swift departure when a man with a gun crept towards them.

Newcastle Waters station, managed by Mr. Burkit for Sir Sidney Kidman and Mr. Lewis, is known to abound in birds which had crowded into the waters as the neighbouring claypans, waterholes and billabongs had dried up. It is the biggest watercourse between Newcastle and Adelaide. The homestead, with a small paddock on its right and a large stockyard behind, faced the waters, which were very low, and of the colour and consistency of artichoke soup, but with a different flavour. People get used to the taste, and find ordinary water insipid after it. One or two of the engineering party, however, were down with some complaint, either due to bathing in the " white water," or else drinking it. Pelicans flew in couples overhead, incredibly high; and upon the lake's dusty banks various long-legged water birds of the crane description were standing, wrapped in meditation. One of the station party, young Mr. Langdon, was good enough to lend me a rifle. The spoonbills were wading in couples, thrashing the water as rhythmically as mowers with scythes, but I could not get near them. The driver of the car had told me what nice purse bags he had made from the spoonbill's bill, saying it was as white as ivory, but these spoonbills had black bills.

Here I saw how the interesting greenhide beds and chairs are made. The bullock skin is simply stretched upon a waggon wheel until the sun has dried it, then a small circle is cut out of it with a knife, and the remaining hide is cut round and round in one long thong about an inch wide, and after it has been pulled out straight it loses any tendency to curl.

The men were branding in the stockyard, and came in to supper relating how the big white calf had put them all up the fence. We spent a very" civilized" evening playing" coon can."

We set off by buggy and a team of five, Mailman MacGregor driving, with a horse-back passenger whom the mailman addressed as Stonewall Jack, and a black boy in charge of a mob of eighteen spare horses.

One of the horses was rather a curiosity. Its owner said that it was "sun-dried"- had been over-heated while being broken in, and had been afraid of a bit of work ever since. It looked like an animated rocking-horse, for its skin was stretched tightly over its ribs, without any suppleness at all. It reminded me of the stuffed horse to be seen at the Waldstein Palace at the Hradschin, near Prague, on whose back the great Count (immortalized by Schiller in "Wallenstein") used to ride up and down the palace staircase.

At midday we halted at the southern end of Stuart's Plain, a good stretch of rising ground about sixteen miles across, which is supposed to have the pecu¬liarity of appearing to be uphill from every point. At night we camped at the Number Seven Bore, beyond the grave of Lindsay Crawford, one of a Government party, who died here in 1901. There was a thunderstorm in the evening, and a tiny but exhilarating shower, the first rain I had seen since leaving Adelaide.

# 6

*My hold of the Colonies is in the close affection which grows from common names, from kindred blood, from similar privileges, and from equal protection. These are ties which, though light as air, are as strong as iron*
- BURKE

AT one station, where the nearest house was thirty miles to the south, and the next nearest sixty miles to the north, and the dwellers to east and west so many hundred miles away that they were altogether out of ken, a man told me that a friend of his had been to. London, and returned saying that there were "miles of roofs." And he laughed as if to say, "There is no accounting for the way some people exaggerate." I told him that it was true, but he only raised his eyebrows and gave a doubtful shake of his head.

While travelling with the camels I had slept on the ground very comfortably, following the fashion of the country, and scooping a little hole for the hip-joint, so that a mattress is not necessary. But now that snakes were getting numerous, I was advised to take a " stretcher," or camp cot.

"We don't mind sleeping on the ground," said one of the hardy spirits. "You see, we're used to it, and if we wake up and find a snake going over us, we lie quite still, and then it doesn't bite. You, maybe, would give a start, and then you might get bitten."

As I felt quite sure that if I woke up and found a snake going over me I should give a very bad start, I accepted the loan of the stretcher. One of the party scorned snakes.

"Take some Condy's Crystals with you," he said, "and if you get bitten, cut out the bite and put in some crystals, and you'll be all right in a few hours. At the worst snake-bite's an easy death. It's those scorpions I can't contend with!"

All this country is considered good pasture, though the rainfall is so uncertain that there is a perpetual danger of cattle dying of want. The average rainfall increases as one goes north, and I was told that the tropical showers of Darwin are measured by feet. In a few weeks' time the grass grows to a height of sixteen feet, but the rank growth is not much use to cattle, and breeds a plague of tormenting flies. Also this grass fruits in a dangerous seed that can pierce the skin of man or beast like a fish hook. At the right season, however, two or three inches of rain, followed a week later by another inch, spells prosperity. It struck me as very strange that in spite of the dry earth and parched trees, the country does not look desolate, and I think this is because the bare trodden earth is harrowed by many cloven feet, which gives it to English eyes the appearance of tillage. The words "Dead Heart," which I often heard used, though they came strangely from the lips of people who refused to call any part of their country a desert, truly describe it, but it only waits a shower to bring it to life.

Our next night was spent at Milliner's, another bore with windmill, trough and tank, where a leakage had nurtured a patch of grass upon which the horses crowded. The mailman, the only regular passer-by, regulates the flow of water.

A day of great heat followed, and the scrubby trees, lancewood, bullwaddy and the picturesque quinine bush, gave no shade at all. At MacGorery's Bore, where we made our dinner camp, the sun was so scorching that the mailman and Stonewall Jack, both of whom looked after my comfort in every possible way, spread a coat under the waggon, the only shady spot, and laid my place there.

Farther on we saw a native's grave up in a tree, like an enormous bird's-nest. This was just before sunset, and there was still light enough to take a photograph. I did not need the mailman's advice not to go too near. One of the terrible rites of the natives in these parts is to light a fire under a corpse that has been "buried" in a tree, and sit round until moisture drips from the body above them, and with this they anoint themselves, rubbing vigorously in the belief that the courage and strength of the dead will thus become their own.

I could not help thinking that the presence of white women in the Northern Territory would do a great deal towards making the natives abandon their dangerous and disgusting customs. All the telegraph stations would make good homes, and if the Government would let land and cattle rights freely to a married stockmaster who undertook to provide the telegraph station with beef and the horse transport necessary for repairing the line, there would very soon be a useful little colony of white men and women and probably children, who would keep up the proper traditions of the Empire.

Just after sunset the buildings of Daley Waters came in sight, and Mr. Holtze offered me the hospitality of the telegraph station.

A surveying party numbering seventeen was encamped here, giving the impression of a dense population.

We made our dinner camp next day at Ironstone, where I could watch the birds clamouring round the water trough; and at sunset Roderick's Bore was like an aviary, hundreds of little birds of several different kinds-greenbacks, doublebars, redhearts, diamond-birds, and those lovely little beings called Java sparrows-were skimming over the trough and taking a drink on the wing, or holding on to the edge and twisting their necks round to reach the water; and the fluttering and warbling and joyousness of these tiny, pretty creatures, after a long day spent in the dry, parching Bush, was truly lovely.

Happily the Government has put a stop to the export of live wild birds, in which at one time the Northern. Territory did a thriving trade. I heard terrible stories of a Frenchman who would lie in wait for them at the watering-places, would catch several dozen at a time in a net, kill them by means of a "crusher," and export them to Paris for the trimming of hats, a lucrative employment, as he received for them the sum of 58s. a dozen.

Next day a long morning stage of twenty miles made it necessary for the horses to rest and feed in the afternoon. The stillness of the siesta was broken by the unusual sound of a car, and Mr. Morris, the engineer of the new railway bridge over the Katherine River, and his assistant, appeared, and offered to drive me on to Maranboy, a hundred and twenty miles north.

So I said good-bye to the mail for four days, and a run of about an hour brought us to the Number One Bore, where we pitched camp.

The place was thronged with bower-birds, which were very amusing to watch, for besides having a sense of humour, these birds also possess the artistic temperament. They make playgrounds wherein to disport themselves, and ornament them with coloured stones, leaves, bits of tin and shells, that they sometimes bring from long distances. There is a yarn that some little nuggets in a bower-bird's playground led to the discovery of a gold-mine.

Mr Holtze was part of the first Northern Territory Expedition, seen here in 1880 (*l to r*); Fred Goss, Waldemar Holtze, G.S. Rattray, George Field.

Some Warramunga men search the tree-grave of a kinsman, three days after his death, hoping to find evidence of a bird or beast.

I had only seen one of these playgrounds before, near Prowse's Gap, not far from Alice Springs, which I found in a dense clump of bushes. The shells were so large (I think some sort of land snail), that I doubted a bird being able to carry them. Macumba Jack, however, told me the place was a "bird's house," and showed me the mound where he said the bird sat, but he did not know the name of the bird, and to all my suggestions replied "Nother sort"; but on this occasion rabbit bones had been the chief medium of the artist. At the Number One, however, the birds were flying about by the score, and their antics at the water trough were very amusing. There were also squatter and bronze-wing pigeons, and the beautiful dollar bird, which is renowned for its lovely blue plumage.

The hundred-mile drive from Number One to Maranboy gave me a very interesting day, even though Bush life fled and flew at the approach of the car. We passed the Warlock, where the mailman had a large camp of horses. Ibis and spoonbills were fishing in a deep water-hole among blue waterlilies.

We came to the old Elsey station, with its demolished homestead and the grave of its master, Mr. Aeneas Gunn, whose wife Jeannie wrote a book called *We of the Never-Never,* read by every person, I should think, who has lived in the Northern Territory.

We passed the Government Experimental Station at Mataranka, where the celebrated £3,000 pumpkin was grown (but I think they can grow on there more cheaply now), and also where the disastrous experiment of keeping sheep in high-grass country was tried, and other schemes of like nature.

We lunched near Bitter Springs at a water-hole on the Roper River at a very tropical spot, among high grass and pandanus trees. I put up one of the big red kangaroo peculiar to the district. Parrots of different sorts abounded all the way, and here there were flocks of the beautiful crimson-wing. The afternoon's run was chiefly along the banks of the King and Roper Rivers. We had now left the parching heat behind, and reached the humidity of watered country. Happily we were spared flies, which I was told become really trying, and necessitate meals under nets.

There were several white people living near Maranboy. The two Sisters in charge of the Australian Inland Mission were most genial and kind,

The Gunn's Elsey Station, as it was in 1895.

Bett-Bett, Jeannie Gunn's help-mate ; *The Little Black Princess*.

and I had a very pleasant time with them. One only wishes that there were more of these hostels, for the plan is certainly a good one. Two ladies, who know each other well enough to feel that they will be good comrades even during two years in the Bush, and who have had a certain amount of nurse's training, sign on for two years, agreeing to run a small hospital and social centre for the benefit of the white people of the district.

The mail from Borrolooloo, on the Gulf of Carpentaria, had brought a passenger for the Katherine. Again I heard tales of travel in the "wet." One of the mailmen, whose contract was worth £300 a year, had to keep sixty horses of his own for mail transport. He had been held up for three days on the bank of a creek, wet to the skin, had lost three horses from bogging or drowning, and was then fined £5 by the "paternal Government" for being late with the mail.

Speaking of being held up, Mailman Macgregor told me that he had had rather a bad experience the previous Christmas, having to wait for five days on the bank of an overflowing creek, short of food, and with no dry camping-place, the fire being lit on the top of a heap of stones, which was built up higher and higher as the water rose. On these occasions there is nothing to do but to wait, opinions being unanimous that there are more deaths from drowning while trying to swim creeks than from exposure to the sun or losing one's way.

The scenery around Maranboy is very pretty, a long, well-watered valley making an oasis. The Sisters brought me here for picnics, and with pleasant conversation and books the time passed very quickly.

Occasionally a patient arrived for treatment, or a wayfarer, who had been far from civilization, would turn up to borrow a book, and to pay his respects to the Sisters.

Everyone knows that the Bush is the place for reflection, and people who spend their lives trying to find the foot of the rainbow (which they expect will materialize in a gold-mine) give one the benefit of their meditations; to-day's Great Thought, from the lips of an old prospector, being, "Aristocracy is the bloom of plebeian selfishness."

The Maranboy policeman was one of the search-party that sailed in the steamer *Huddersfield* in search of two white women supposed to be the sole survivors of a shipwreck on the shores of the Gulf of Carpentaria. They

Topsy alighted and caught a sand-devil, a little animal that looked like a large toad, but walked like a lizard, and was clothed in a were said to have fallen into the hands of the natives. The expedition suffered a good deal of privation, and did a good deal of hard work, but it achieved nothing. It was concluded that the women must have been drowned at sea, since there was no trace of them. The matter still remains a mystery, and it is doubtful whether the truth about them will ever be known.

We started off again with fresh horses and a passenger from Queensland on the last two days of our journey through the Bush. After a twenty-four-mile run we camped at Rockhole, a pretty spot where the water lies under a cliff, and a flock of pigeons came down under the rock to drink. There was another camper here, on his way south from Emungalen, who sent us over a large bag of lemons, a gift that was generous, as well as refreshing, as citrus fruits have to come by sea. We made an early start, and crossed Maude's Creek and the Bullock's Head, where we saw gorgeous parrots in large flocks. Twice we met men travelling with buggies, and once a team of thirty-seven donkeys hauling a six-ton load from the railway to a remote cattle station, a journey that they accomplished twice a year. The little animals all looked in fine condition. They had neither rein nor bridle, but responded to the voices and whip-crack of their white master and his black helper.

A group of natives approached, to pass the time of day. One of them was known as a rain-maker. On being chaffed upon the futility of his profession he told us his method. He got a bowl of clean water, put a clean white stone in it, poured some more water over it, and sat down and waited for the rain. But this time the rain had not come, and he was at a loss to account for his failure. He was now begging the mailman for a " bit of flour and a bit of meat," for he, his little brother, and his blind friend were all very hungry. "All true," he remarked. "I not gammon mailman."

There were some good trees growing by the way-side: Morton Bay ash, kurrajong, bloodwood, coola-bar, snappy gum (in demand for baking damper), and gutta-percha, whose milky juice is so dangerous that a splash in the eye will cause blindness.

In the dry country tiny stingless bees, coming in little clouds, covered our arms; and ants, black, white, yellow, red, and green, whose dwellings vary from small cup-like houses near the ground to "beds" eighteen or twenty feet high, with "meridian" tendencies, were a daily problem.

So far, the meridian ant has baffled scientific explanation. Just as the Chinese can "smell the north," so does the meridian ant possess some instinct concerning the Pole.

The Queensland passenger proved himself an acquisition, for the five horses, which had pulled the buggy over fallen tree-trunks and up and down rocks as a matter of course, took fright at a sheet of bark lying in the road and bolted. They had some cause for fear, for the near leader trotted over its edge and it upped and slapped him. They raced into the Bush at full gallop, and tore through the scrub. Our safety depended on whether they could be got back to the road before they reached a tree that stood at the edge of a thickly wooded bit of country. The mailman handed one of the ribbons to the Queenslander, and they each wrapped a rein round their hands and pulled. We returned to the road again without anyone being hurt, but there was time for a good thrill before the horses could be persuaded to return and work off their excitement in a safer place. The little incident gave rise to some excellent stories of runaways and other adventures.

Old deserted gold-diggings, where fossickers had been trying their luck, flanked the road, but they had never been profitable. We followed the trend of the Maude Ranges, driving almost south, and it was a change to have the sun on one's back, instead of dazzling one's eyes. We halted for dinner at the Five Mile Hole, where we met another traveller - the fifth in two days.

Small holdings of land were being taken up on the banks of the Katherine, and the district looked prosperous and settled. There were flowering trees, ponchiana and frangipani, and others not indigenous to the country. An effort was being made at orange and banana growing. The waters of the river were clear and beautiful, and must have been appreciated by the horses, which for many days had drunk only of the dregs of water-holes and billabongs.

We stopped at the post office with the mails, and the postmaster handed me telegrams, and gave me tea in his cool verandah looking over the river.

Mrs. Morris had asked me to stay with her until "train day," which, owing to the increase of traffic caused by the bridge works, was now once a week instead of fortnightly. So I said farewell to the mailman and my fellow-passengers - trusty friends of the road-and had a pleasant little visit to Mrs. Morris at Emungalen in her comfortable house built on piles, with stump-caps to check the depredations of the white ants. Mrs. Morris is a niece of Mr. George Lambert, the great Australian painter whose portraits have created interest in both hemispheres.

The socialistic tendencies of the Northern Territory were brought home to me when I heard that the hundred-and-ninety-eight-mile journey from Emungalen to the coast was not accomplished by rail in one day. At the Edith River and the Ferguson white men were working on the. railway, and I was surprised, in such a climate, to see a white stoker on the engine of the train. Passengers were set down to spend the night at Pine Creek, a flourishing little township with a hospital and hotel, which miners and prospectors seemed chiefly to inhabit. The proprietress of the hotel had lived here in days before the natives had become reconciled to the presence of white men, and as soon as the third sitting at dinner was over (for surveyors, prospectors, and railway men on their way to Darwin for the monthly steamer caused a good deal of congestion) she came and chatted to me of her very interesting early experiences among the blacks.

An early start was made, and the train meandered on its way through varying country: the bareness of the Union Mine Siding, Boomalera, Borrundie, Brock's Creek and the trickle of water at the Adelaide River, Rum Jungle, so called from the amount of rum sold to thirsty fossickers, through straight-stemmed Bush, clumps of pandanus trees and bamboo. There was very little attempt at cultivation, but at one place we were able to buy melons from a garden. Occasionally we saw a water-hole belonging to a cattle station, and then came gradually past infrequent grey roofs to clusters of buildings and flowering trees, until, as we neared the outskirts of Darwin, a gap in the landscape gave me my first view of the sea - a stretch of blue dancing water under the hot, milky

Cavanagh Street, Darwin's "Chinatown", as I saw it.

Chinese workers on Cavanagh Street, Darwin, about 1922.

white sky. And I realized that the life of wide spaces, open sky, patriarchal simplicity-all that the word "Bush" had meant to me-were things of the past, and the journey was over.

Now that I can look back upon the journey as a whole, the things that stand out are the wide spaces and baking heat; the small tearing sound with which the gum-trees strip off slivers of their bark in the hot silence of noon; the glamour of the sunset, and the benison of the evening breeze; the sudden meetings with men and occasionally women who, by no means rendered either dull-witted or nervous by their isolation, were, on the contrary, frequently well-read and versed in the affairs of the day. Their hospitality, of course, is proverbial, but I found besides that an unfailing friendliness, which alone made it possible for a stranger to travel across the continent from sea to sea, and to arrive with so many pleasant memories.

Somebody said that Darwin was like a shop with all its soiled goods in the window; certain it is that one hears the worst of it, but none of the best of it, long before one arrives there.

One man remarked, "The south would faint if it knew what happens in Darwin."

I am inclined to think that the south is made of sterner stuff, and that it would not faint, but would lend a stronger helping hand.

The place is extraordinarily hot - said to be the hottest in the world - and it is difficult not to be idle. All the problems that appear to be simple ones at Alice Springs have grown very complicated by the time that one arrives in Darwin. There is a China Town, and also a "Greekman Town." The sole industry (apart from the handling of some four hundred tons of cargo for the two ships a month) is in connection with the meat-works, which pays high wages during the few months in the year that it is open.

But I can only speak of Darwin as I found it.

Like other parts of Australia it is a place of great hospitality and pleasant friendships. The Administrator and Mrs. Urquhart were very kind to me, I saw Darwin under the auspices of Professor Watson and Dr. Leighton-Jones and I felt that I could not have had better friends.

I wonder. now that I should ever have been surprised, in the early days of my travels, to find how English the people of Australia are.

On the long journey a group of people asked me, "What do you think of Australia, and what do you think of us?" And I told them, "I think you're so English."

Their reply gave me a feeling of pride.

"That's what we like to be," they said. "Of course, we're all Australians, and proud of it, and some of us are Irish, and some are Scotch and so forth, but we all like to think of ourselves as Englishmen."

My wayside friends entertained just a tired traveller, but I was meeting staunch, loyal types of the sons of the Empire, keenly alive, thinkers and men of action. I felt the bond that united us at the first handclasp, and when I found, as I very frequently did find, that they had fought in the War, of course the bond was doubly strong.

This account of various journeys is necessarily both slight and incomplete, for I did not set out with the idea of writing about them, but of travelling for my own pleasure and education, glad to have an opportunity of gaining a little first-hand knowledge of this very important part of the Empire.

Yet the writing of it has been a pleasure, for to some extent I have lived these journeys over again, and met again - if only in the realms of memory - men and women whose friendship I shall always prize.

I owe them my thanks, not only for their kindness to me, but for what they taught me.

Hands across the sea!

Getting through. Kathleen Howell placing long strips of coconut matting under the wheels of Jean Anderson's Lancia Lamda, on the road from Oodnadatta to Alice Springs, 1927.

www.ingramcontent.com/pod-product-compliance
Lightning Source LLC
Chambersburg PA
CBHW050820090426
42737CB00021B/3452